The first Spanish edition of ***Sammy Sosa en 9 Innings*** was published in 1999. It was placed on the first suggested reading list of the millennium compiled by Connecting Libraries and School Project (CLASP), sponsored by the NYC Board of Education, The School of Library Services, the Brooklyn Public Library, The New York Public Library and The Queens Borough Public Library.

The NYC Board of Education included ***Sammy Sosa en 9 Innings*** on its list of texts and reference materials for its students.

These are some commentaries from educators and the Spanish media, about the book and its author.

"One hopes that all our students would have the opportunity to read this kind of book. It teaches and inspires them so much, and will definitly be a strong and positive influence in their lives."

Frank Cortorreal
Roberto Clemente Middle School/The Bronx

"J.C. Malone's presentation was directly related to the lives of my students. He touched upon the immigrant experience in a fun and thought-provoking way."

Tara Gualtieri
Washington Irving High School/Manhattan

"***Sammy Sosa en 9 Innings*** was the number one best-seller last week in the Spanish bookstores of New York. Its author relates the political, economic and social history of his country of origin with that of the United States since the beginning of the 20th Century."

Adalberto Domínguez
Hoy/Santo Domingo, Dominican Republic

"***Sammy Sosa en 9 Innings*** establishes itself as one of the most complete works in contemporary baseball."

Constantino Viloria-
El Diario/La Prensa/New York

"This biography is like a flea market. You will find a lot of different, interesting and strange stuff."

Miriam Ventura
Hoy/New York

"It takes us by the hand to a point where we understand the meaning of Sammy's figure, not only for the Dominicans but for all Latin Americans."

Adriana Carrera
Tiempos del Mundo/New York

"It is not only the story of Sammy Sosa's hardship and good luck, but the story of a whole country, of many generations of a small village, part of the history of the United States, Latin America and even of each and every one of us."

Santiago Gutiérrez
Universal Prensa/ New York

"It is so much more than a… biography. It is a review of the history of baseball that is closely related to the very history of the Dominican Republic."

Mario Rodríguez-El Siglo/
Santo Domingo, Dominican Republic.

Sammy Sosa in 9 Innings

Julio C. Malone

Professor Gregg View
from the English Department of
Grand Valley State University
edited this book

Editorial Miglo

2005

First Spanish Edition 1999

Original Spanish title: Sammy Sosa en 9 Innings

Photo Credits:
Cover:
The Associated Press and Dominican Archives
Interior:
Polín Jiménez,
Author's Photo:
Solángel Valdez

Library of Congress Catalog Card Number 2003092899
ISBN # 0-9671705-1-6

Editorial Miglo
1560 Grand Concourse #504
Bronx, NY. 10457
www.edimiglo.com

Cover and Design
Ramón Peralta

Table of Contents

Dedication

To my parents, Joseph and Isabel Malone,
two West Indies immigrants
who wound up in Consuelo
before departing to their
very own promised land:
eternity.

Introduction to the English Edition

Stories are among the best ways to learn about the wit and wisdom of any culture. By giving us a deeper understanding of our real identity, stories can help us become who we want to be.

Working as a high school teacher and curriculum development consultant, I observed something disturbing. Our Hispanic young adults have very few stories to which they can personally relate, and obtain the rich wit and wisdom of Hispanic culture.

In baseball Hispanics, especially Dominicans, have excelled the most in contemporary American society; many of my fellow villagers are among the shiniest stars in the game. Here I have compiled some of their stories, weaving them into the broader scheme of things in the Dominican, American and Latin American life.

This book contains a kind of a treasure map of these ball players journey to success, with hints and points of reference that our youth, and adults, can use in their lives.

New York City's educational community gave the first Spanish edition of ***Sammy Sosa en 9 Innings*** a very warm reception. School districts and libraries have bought the book and invited me to address their students. Parents have told me that they used it as family readings; many students have written me letters saying they enjoyed and learned from the book.

In classrooms and auditoriums of public schools and public libraries across New York City I have been asked, time and again, for the English translation.Readers eagerly bought the first Spanish edition in bookstores, churches, barbershops, beauty parlors and grocery stores.

It has been, indeed, quite an exciting ride, with many

twists and turns. One particular part of this trip, nevertheless, almost spoiled the entire ride. That morning I had no idea of what to say just minutes before talking to students from Union High School, in Grand Rapids, Michigan. I shivered inside, my heart beating fast. I was afraid, but not insecure as I approached the microphone.

The Grand Rapids Public Schools is trying to bring more equity to their classrooms, curriculum and learning environment, and brings the students inspiring Hispanic stories as part of that effort. Union principal Ms. Janice Johnson, the director of the District's English Language Learners Department, Mr. Roberto Saenz and School Board secretary Mr. Luis Peña invited me to address and inspire their Hispanic students. But something awfully wrong happened.

Sammy's corked bat had just broken a couple of days before; to talk about that fellow's achievements, integrity, and honorability no longer seemed like a very good idea. A high school was the wrong place, he was the wrong person and those days were definitely the wrong time.

I got up and walked toward the podium, trusting the universe to provide me with the right words to deliver a constructive message to the kids.

Sammy's corked bat and the scandal involving Danny Almonte, The Bronx Superstar pitcher of the Little League World Series 2001, happened after the first Spanish edition of this book was published.

A new appendix to this First English Edition includes the thoughts I shared with the students of Union High School. It also includes a public yet personal letter I've addressed to Danny Almonte, the shiniest rising star of Dominican baseball.

My hope is that Danny, our young men and women—and all who look to baseball and other sports as a way to stay young at heart—learn from disappointments and painful moments and keep fighting to become all they want to be.

Acknowledgments

Teamwork

I wanted to dedicate this book to my daughters Mabel, Isabel, Gloria, and Lillian, but I figured out that would not make any sense. While this work was in progress, they behaved better than any girls in the entire world. I can't remember a moment when they did anything to break my concentration and dedication to this project. I locked myself up for long hours with the computer while they were reading, studying, listening to music or doing whatever they could to entertain themselves, despite no TV or video games. They were always supportive, understanding, loving and very helpful. The family wrote this book. We all invested time, energy, patience, understanding and sacrifice in this work. That is why it would not make any sense to dedicate the book to them.

They are co-authors.

My eternal debt of gratitude to Delight Lester, for her support.

My co-workers at *El Diario La Prensa*, New York City's oldest daily Spanish paper, dealt with my ups and downs during this process. All of them, from editor-in-chief Rossana Rosado, to the custodian José Santiago, have my honest, deepest and sincere gratitude.

My colleague, Constantino Viloria, without trying or knowing, became the best librarian with whom I have ever worked. Without his support, this book would have been incomplete. My sincere gratitude to Carlos Julio Díaz, Nieves González, Wilson Vargas, Fernando A. de León and my sister Gloria Malone. Without them, this would have been a collection of mistakes. Any mistakes found here, are my own responsibility.

Doctor Félix Casas and Luis Leonor did whatever they

could to see that this work would read as a piece of art. My special gratitude to Milito Peralta, my graphic designer, who discovered in the process that he actually had a lot more patience than he was willing to admit.

I was very fortunate to be able to count on a great team, with players like Manny Acta in Florida, Juan Francisco Vilorio and Wilfredo Polanco in the Dominican Republic. My deepest gratitude to all of those who have helped me so much and know me so well that they don't feel bad because their names aren't here. They know I carry them deep inside my heart.

This English version is possible thanks to a community of good friends with kind hearts, open minds, observant eyes and helping hands. María Eugenia Marino-Hidalgo, in Twin Cities, Minnesota, provided invaluable guidance with the first draft.

Then came the ecumenical touch, from the Reverend Cannon Ricardo Potter, Associated Director of the Office of Anglican and Global Relations in downtown Manhattan. Then father Steve Cron, rector of the Roman Catholic Saint John's Parish, to Reverend Bruce A. Bode from the Liberal Fountain Street Church, to Dr. Donald Lester, a retired Presbyterian minister, all in Grand Rapids Michigan.

Deb Zoppa, from St. Thomas the Apostol High School in Rockford, Michigan, gave me invaluable grammar insights.Milca Esdaille in The Bronx, New York, and Judy Allen in Cleveland, Ohio, did a fine editing work.

Dr. Cliff Welch, from the history department of Grand Valley State University in Allendalle, Michigan, was the best friend I could have ever find in the academic community. He provided crucial guidance and support.

My debt of gratitude to my editor Gregg View, from the Grand Valley State University English Department and Allen Teneyck, PhD., a retired university professor.

My special thanks to Jeff Cranson and Linda Miller, from the Grand Rapids Press. For their keen, detail-oriented eyes and gentle souls for understanding.

Thank you very much, Grand Rapids Michigan.

With all my heart and soul.

Julio C. Malone

Introduction

Up until then, I only knew J.C. Malone by his very poignant columns published weekly in *El Diario la Prensa*, New York City's oldest Spanish daily paper. But he always gave me the feeling of being a guy willing to speak his mind with honesty. When we talked for the first time, he gave me strong proof of that. He wanted me to read the manuscript of a book he had written about the life of a sports hero. But he wanted it quick. He asked me to do it as soon as possible. He had never written about this topic, and wanted my feedback.

Well, Malone is one of those guys who think that sportscasters only work a couple of hours during the night. What then do they do with the rest of their time? Well, they are available for any adventure, or to continue talking about baseball, boxing or whatever other sports someone wants to talk about. He does not have it quite right there.

But I decided to do it anyway.

I did not regret it. First, because the book is very well written. Second, because it is not only a story of Sammy Sosa, starting with his days of hardship in the dusty streets of our town and ending with his days of glory. It also talks about the history of baseball in the Dominican Republic, and about the immigrant groups who settled in the sugar plantation. That became a starting point for the development of many sports stars.

Sammy Sosa en 9 Innings will be a bookstore success.

It is a compelling story, very easy to read. It is more than an unauthorized biography of the popular ballplayer and his family. At times, it is sad and raw. Other times, it's charming and funny. But above all, it's deeply human.

With his poignant style, Malone portrays the life in the

bateyes (villages in the sugar cane plantations). He opens a window for us to see the exploitation by the owners of the estates, the incredible way of life of the immigrants and their indisputable integrity. Malone spent his childhood years in the Ingenio Consuelo, making him an eyewitness to many aspects of the story he is telling us. He knows what he is talking about. He knew the very formation of the character of his community.

He talks about famous old social clubs such as Club Los Laureles, and about the infamous Barrio Lindo in San Pedro de Macorís. In his story, even the devil himself jumps out of the pages as a character. I sincerely think that whoever knows San Pedro de Macorís and its sugar estates will feel a little nostalgic.

Regarding Sammy Sosa, I have no doubt that Malone has hit the nail on the head. He has hit the ball in the face. He talks about a man who has openly spoken about his humble origin and his years of abject poverty, a man who has been very honest about his life. Malone has managed to take us by the hand through his tormented but triumphant adventure.

I am sure that ***Sammy Sosa en 9 Innings*** will engage you, as it did me.

I want to make something clear: J.C. Malone didn't catch me off base. From the very first moment in which we spoke, I knew that I would enjoy his friendship and his talent.

Billy Berroa
New York Mets' Spanish Sportscaster

This is where I came from
I passed this way.
This should not be shameful
Or hard to say
A self is a self
It is not a screen

A person should respect
What he has been
This is my past
Which I shall not discard
This is the ideal
This is hard

James Fenton

Warming Up

Deep Into the Plantation

Don Luis, the owner and chauffeur of the small Peugeot taxi that we were getting in, was a little overweight, just as my parents were. Once we entered the car, my five sisters, my brother and I squeezed against one another or sat on each other's laps, filling in the spaces the grown-ups left.

After a few attempts, we did it!

The doors were closed, and Don Luis started the car. As it moved from side to side, in and out of the potholes in the road, we adjusted to one another, squashed as sardines in a can, but happy and hopeful.

We drove about five miles on the curved asphalt road, dug up among many cane fields, resembling a giant black snake. Many stops were necessary, yielding to trains dragging wagons filled with sugarcane or carts pulled by bulls with the same cargo. Some fields were totally cut and others were in the works.

On that sunny Sunday afternoon, the air was sweet and musical, filled with the scent of fresh cut sugarcane, and the rhythm of the Haitian workers, who were chanting in Creole while working the fields.

After about 15 minutes, we got to Estadio Tetelo Vargas in San Pedro de Macorís, the home of our local professional baseball team: "Estrellas Orientales."

We were attending the last game of the final playoffs, "D-Day;" the championship was decided in that Dominican baseball season. It was February 14th, Valentine's Day, 1968, and Sammy Sosa would be born nine months later.

We arrived at the stadium filled with hope, and we left pregnant with pride. Our Estrellas Orientales won the championship and three of the stars were our fellow villagers. One of our boys, Ricardo Carty, drove the fans crazy with his performance. Another, Rafael –*El Gallo*– (The Rooster) Batista, scored the winning run. That day we consueleros were united by a great sense of pride. Our boys won the National Championship.

It was our victory.

Consuelo is the name of our batey (village), located deep in the plantation, in a literally nonexistent space between the cane fields and the mill.

I was ten when that game and baseball captivated my imagination. I was mesmerized in front of the TV screen with Dagoberto –*Bert*– Campaneris, the Oakland Athletics' shortstop. He didn't run after the grounders; he danced after them with artistic elegance.

A chain of events nurtured my baseball dreams.

Carty was a family friend and dropped by to visit with my parents, a couple of British West Indies immigrants, or Cocolos, as our group is called. That day he gave me my first ball. Then Jesús –*Pepe*– Frías passed by and gave me another one. The boyfriend of one of my sisters, a newly signed professional pitcher, gave me the third one. I managed to get a bat, a glove, uniform and spikes; my decision was made.

I was going to be a ballplayer.

I would play shortstop as elegantly as Campaneris, and all the girls in the batey and beyond would go crazy for me. One afternoon, after school, I took my sports apparel and gear, and set out for the diamond to encounter my destiny of fame, fortune and stardom.

Since my debut in the batting box, the fans made me understand things with their clear, spontaneous and honest commentaries.

"Pitch it again, he didn't see it," they would tell the pitcher.

"Hey, tell your dad to buy you glasses," they told me.

"That one went by at night time. He didn't even see it!"

"That guy is so bad he would beat up his mama on Mother's Day," they made fun of me.

"That good-for-nothing could not even hit a green coconut. Get him out of there!" they demanded.

I cried, but deep inside. Outwardly I kept calm. Stoic.

I was a clumsy kid with a total lack of motor coordination, incapable of calculating the distance and speed of the ball. Very seldomly would my bat and the ball meet. When they did, the impact shook my whole body. It made me feel as if all the little needles in the world were coming out of my hands, pinching me from the inside. I trembled as if I had Parkinson's disease.

As a defensive player, I was a lot better.

Since my dad and my grandpa were Evangelical ministers, I bragged about being well connected in the heavens. When I got to play shortstop, I prayed in silence that no one hit the ball my way. And my prayers were answered most of the time.

My hopeful journey to intended stardom was not an easy one. It was a rocky climb. I was allowed to play on that team for different reasons than the other players. They never had even the slightest hope about my future as a baseball player. They needed my bat, glove and balls. Owning equipment kept me in the game. Players such as –Marino– the nickname we had for Julio César Franco, had to come out of the game every now and then to let me play.

In school, the boy sitting behind me was a bit old for the grade. There wasn't then, and still is not, social promotion in the Dominican Republic. This guy had such a distracted, absent-minded air, as if waiting for answers to transcendental questions that he never asked.

"What the heck am I doing here?" I imagined was the question Bacá asked himself. Bacá was his nickname. Ball players seem to born with nicknames.

He never knew what was being discussed in class or what the teachers were talking about, and showed no interest whatsoever in finding out. He was the kind of guy you would approach and knock on his broad forehead with your knuckles before asking: "Is anybody home?"

In the morning, we walked together because he lived half way between my home and the school. It really didn't matter how distracted he seemed to be, Bacá never allowed any grownup to abuse me or the other kids in the class. For a bunch of us lacking physique and courage, he was the protector, the big brother.

One day it seemed as if he found the answer he was waiting for, or perhaps he got sick and tired of waiting and decided to chase it. When we got to the school's gate, he kept right on going, straight up to the baseball diamond across from the schoolyard.

He was the shortstop I wanted to be.

In the field, he danced just as Campaneris did and maybe with a lot more artistic flexibility; in fact, the guy looked more like a dancer than a ballplayer. It was not long before an American team signed him up and took him away from Consuelo. Bacá was known worldwide by his full name –Alfredo Griffin– when he became the American League Rookie of the Year in 1979.

A lot of my friends and classmates were signed up to play pro ball, and many of them made it to the Majors. Thanks to their skills on the diamond, even before becoming professional players, all the girls in the village were dreaming of them. After coming back home at the end of a season in the United States, the entire batey focused its collective attention on them. They were fortunate in the game and fortunate in love.

Human worth was measured in that world by one's baseball abilities. Excellence in baseball was a rite of passage to manhood, and after failing it shamefully, I was at a disadvantage. In Consuelo, every boy who was anybody was a good ball player.

I was a nobody.

Baseball closed for me the doors that were opened to others. After a couple of seasons without hitting the ball, and afraid of catching it, I figured out that I could not become a ballplayer.

I accepted the fans' unsolicited advice.

I retired from baseball. One afternoon I walked off the diamond and went to visit my Aunt Syntia, who lived close by. I noticed she had abandoned the idea of having a flower garden in her frontyard. The flowers were covered with dust stirred up by trucks loaded with sugarcane passing in front of her house all the time.

Instead of a flower garden, she had a controlled little

jungle. Between the flower garden that never was and the Club Los Laureles beside her home, I abandoned forever the glove, the bat, balls, uniform and baseball dreams.

Then I did what any sane person would have done: I changed my plans, returning to my life's first dream, one that perhaps I should have never abandoned. It came about at the Anglican parochial school where I learned to read and write. While the teachers would take a break, called "Social Friday," we, the students, amused them with our artistic talents.

Besides having a physical handicap for baseball, I was born with an inability to articulate the "R" sound. Despite being media lengua ("half a tongue," they called me) I was a very famous singer.

Every Friday, fans from all over the school and beyond would come to my classroom to hear me sing. Receiving standing ovations was the regular beginning of my weekend.

I didn't perform as a soloist but as part of a duo with a classmate who stuttered. He was gago, as we called it in Spanish.

The fans and critics agreed that, as a duo, we were unique, the only duet formed by guys with speech impediments. The gago and the medio lengua would be the name of our duet. We would have been, according to them, undisputedly famous.

I thought about going back to this idea because, after all, girls fall more for singers than ballplayers. An ironic detail ruined my road to artistic stardom: Rodrigo Velonny, my stuttering duet partner, was an excellent shortstop and he signed up to play pro ball.

Baseball sabotaged my artistic career.

But I had to survive and rescue my self-esteem.

I devoted myself to a secret project: The organization of an opposition party against baseball. I would assemble other kids disinherited from the sport. We would discuss the uselessness of baseball and the emptiness of its senseless reality. Above all, we would agreed on how stupid it was to devote one's entire life to chasing a ball that another stupid guy hit with a stick.

You tell me: What sense does that make?

I sought refuge in reading.

I became a little bookworm, one of those who devoured the pages of old books. To avoid having to face the shameful reality of being a pitiful ballplayer, I would spend all the time with my head between the pages of any book. Books saved me from feeling the indifference that girls showed toward unimportant fellows like me. Books opened a whole new world for me. They helped me escape from the chimney of the sugar factory that rose as my unavoidable destiny, after the destruction of my artistic and sporting dreams.

As time went by, I noticed that baseball changed the lives of many of my childhood friends. It was, indeed, the best thing that ever happened to Consuelo and the Dominican Republic.

Sammy Sosa and his performance in the 1998 season made me revisit that past. He was born across from my Aunt Syntia's yard where I abandoned my baseball dreams.

The same baseball that yesterday rejected me now brings me back to write this story. At times, I believe that baseball pushed me away a long time ago, trying to make it harder for me to work on this story today.

While researching Sammy Sosa's story, I returned to Consuelo, found my roots, those of the batey and the mysterious relationship between baseball, religion and nature. Three strikes, three outs, three bases; like Christianity, the whole game rests on a rule of three.

It is a trilogy, similar to Christianity's trinity.

The number three, multiplied by itself equals nine; the game has nine innings, there are nine players on a team and, perhaps the most important thing, there are nine months between conception and birth.

Perhaps baseball is that invisible frontier where humankind, nature and religion get together. As in any frontier, there is a no man's land, a place that runs according to its own rules, against all conventionalism, a place where incredible and mysterious things happen.

All the time.

1st Inning

Top of the First

Horse of Mysteries

He jumps up and for a few seconds seems to be suspended in the air, with his fists closed tight, as if he is holding onto something invisible, powerful. Extending his sight across the field, he sees the ball clear the fence. He lands with his index and middle fingers forming the sign of victory, bringing them to his lips and, through them, blows kisses into the air.

With those fingers he proclaims the victory of friendship over death; he does it in tribute to a friend who recently passed away. The first kiss goes to his mother down in the Dominican Republic; the rest to all the mothers of the world.

Once he finishes that rite, Sammy Sosa, mysterious as a black Stallion, starts his ceremonial trot across the diamond, stopping time in a magical moment; uniting the crowd in a euphoric spiritual connection. Fans from all over the world, from all teams, races, social classes, political ideologies and religious creeds are united. People from all walks of life, with countless reasons to be divided, come together in this unique moment.

Sammy tours the diamond wrapped in a bubble of ovation. He greets his teammates, who form a line to congratulate him; then he enters the dugout. The fans' applause keeps on going with a life of its own; only he can stop it. He climbs out again, this time as a new living legend of baseball, takes off his cap and waves it in the air as a magic wand. The cheering increases before it fades into a deep silence over the stadium.

The game continues.

That Tuesday Sammy waited on three balls; he had two strikes and swung at the sixth pitch; the ball flew over Chicago's Wrigley Field's left field fence and fell straight into history. It was June 30th, 1998, when he hit 20 home runs in one month. No other player has done anything like this since the first home run entered the record books in 1876. It was hit by Ross Barnes of the Chicago White Sox.

Sammy, it is good to know, didn't come out of the blue.

He is the latest and brightest star of a Latin American constellation to shine over the Major Leagues in the past half a century. A good point of departure to trace this story is 1956, when Osvaldo —El Orégano— Virgil became the first Dominican in the Majors. That year Venezuelan Luis Aparicio was the first Latin American to achieve an important honor: Rookie of the Year in the American League.

By 1958, Puerto Rican Orlando —Peruchin— Cepeda, would get the same award. Cuban Tony Oliva and Panamanian Rod Carew would also be selected Rookie of the Year in 1964 and 1967, respectively.

Sammy continued on a path opened by Cuban Zoilo —*El Zorro*— Versalles, the first Latin American chosen Most Valuable Player in the American League in 1965. He is the newest version of Puerto Rican Roberto Clemente, the first Latin American elected the National League MVP in 1966.

Sammy is the most recent example of the great Dominican talent in baseball. He is one of the most important players in the world, discovered by the expert and visionary eyes of another Dominican, Omar Minaya, the first Hispanic to become general manager of a Major League team. It is a combination of that Dominican talent that made Sammy a new baseball star, and the most admired and respected player in the game's recent history.

Admiration for his skills and personality spread like a worldwide fever. As if they had formally agreed upon it, his fans took whitewash paint and decorated a corner of their vehicles' front or rear windshields with "Sosa" followed by a number. In the summer of 1998 this decoration could be seen on many cars, vans and pickup trucks. Every day that number changed, according to how close Sammy got to breaking the records. First the 60 homers in a season that Babe Ruth achieved in 1927, and then 61, set by Roger Maris in 1961.

The numbers after "Sosa" expressed the collective hope

for Sammy to hit his next home run. This feeling unified Dominicans, then all Hispanics, followed by African-Americans, and soon many white Americans. These groups invested a lot of positive energy, providing moral and spiritual support to their first common hero: a black Dominican immigrant, a man who inspired and entertained both the most powerful man in the world, President Bill Clinton, and the poorest street children in the Dominican Republic.

Sosamanía

The police in New York City, under Mayor Rudolph Giulliani's administration, tried to stop the euphoria. They fined motorists for painting on their windshields, claiming that the marks obstructed visibility. Cars with the signs, nevertheless, started multiplying in Washington Heights, the Dominican barrio of Manhattan. They crossed to The Bronx, went down to Harlem, then to Brooklyn and Queens. It was impossible to stop something that was spreading throughout the city, covering the country, and reaching as far as Latin America and Japan. It developed an uncontrollable force, more powerful than the sum of all the goodwill that inspired it and the attempts to stop it.

It was *Sosamanía*.

The greatest expression of care and support for a Latin American player since 1981, when *Fernandomania* developed around Mexican pitcher Fernando Valenzuela. This new force destroyed old fans' loyalties to their teams, instead compelling them to become fans of the game. Everyone went to the stadium hoping to see Sammy hit his next homer, even if it was against their team. They were attending a special moment in the history of baseball and the United States.

That was above all other considerations.

Sammy's rituals and homers, together with Mark McGwire's, were among the few positive things that the United States had going in those days. Politicians had divided the country.

One group of right-wing republicans was taking President Clinton to the political slaughterhouse because of his inappropriate relationship with a young girl; another group supported him.

Both options were awful and, in that moment, Sosamanía united the country around something positive. It was the healthiest and most refreshing option, one of the best reasons to feel national pride. In the Dominican Republic, Sammy's homeland, it helped people to cope with the deep sense of loss and sorrow that remained after opposition leader José Francisco Peña Gómez passed away.

Sosamanía returned to baseball the enchantment lost with strikes and greedy squabbles for money between players and team owners. Its fever bridged the abyss that separated players and fans, since the first became millionaires with money paid by the second.

It exhibited mysterious powers.

Baseball saints Babe Ruth and Roger Maris moved over, opening space on the altar to accommodate Sammy, with fan support, contrary to what had happened in the past. When Maris, a white man, was ready to break Ruth's record in 1961, the fans insulted him for his lack of respect; they even spat on him. Until 1974, no one dared to approach, let alone surpass, Ruth's lifetime record of 714 homers. That year, Hank Aaron, a Black American, was ready to do it. Some of Ruth's die-hard fans threatened to kill him because of his irreverence.

No one wanted those sacred marks to be touched, but *Sosamania* changed that. It is a new standard at the highest level of baseball and a great demonstration of human solidarity. Combining those factors, Sammy emerged as the new star of the greatest American sports show; he became the most admired sports figure, a role model and national hero in several countries.

The New King

Sammy is one of the best things that has happened to baseball since Babe Ruth. He is one of those uncommon characters that grows with humility, a unique player whose personality embodies the very spirit of baseball and transcends the stadium.

On his way to the top of the mountain, he undertook a long, winding, rocky, upward journey. He was born and grew up in abject poverty, with little or no education. During the 1998 season, nevertheless, he conducted himself with natural calm and humble demeanor, to create a positive impression on the fans worldwide.

Maris was a college student when he signed up to play pro ball. In 1961, before breaking Ruth's record of 60 homers, his education did not help him to keep his temper. He couldn't stand the pressure from the fans or the media.

He lived in a constant state of nervous crisis. His hair even fell out.

Ruth played baseball with many advantages that worked against Sammy. The sliders that pitchers use today didn't exist during Ruth's time. No pitcher ever had the opportunity to study a video of Ruth in the batting box to identify his weakness, as they do today with Sammy. Every pitcher in the game has taken the time to study Sammy's batting habits, to decide in advance which pitch works best to neutralize him.

Sammy, similar to Ruth, completed a long journey, from the abyss of extreme poverty to the mountaintop of fame and fortune. The road of the Dominican player, however, was different and maybe worse than Ruth's in many ways: Sammy is an immigrant in a country of immigrants that seemed to have lost its memory and is turning against immigrants. He is a black man in a country that has yet to come to accept racial diversity. Despite these and other obstacles, Sammy is accepted, loved and worshipped as the new idol all across the USA.

Sammy's accomplishment coincides with the first 100 years of baseball in the Dominican Republic. The sport was brought to the country by Cuban refugees at the end of the 19th century.

If Sammy's homers were exciting, his story and the history of baseball in the Dominican Republic is a lot more exciting. His story shows how life chose him and trained him every step of the way up to where he is now.

Baseball in his life is the product of a strange blend of poverty, politics and religion, of hard work, untiring practice, absolute discipline and long hours of study.

Sammy comes from a world where few things are what

they seem to be and seldom look as they really are. It is a strange and mysterious place where reality makes fun of itself and, at moments, becomes fantasy to deceive the imagination. And confuse it.

Polín Jiménez

Omar Minaya, General Manager of the Montreal Expos, is the highest-ranking Dominican in the Major League baseball corporate world. He signed Sammy Sosa, one of the most important players in the game.

Bottom of the First

The Lonely Patriot

The watchman spotted a small rowboat approaching the American destroyer *USS Memphis*, anchored outside the harbor of Santo Domingo, the country's capital city. Morning had just broken, a new day was born as the sun rose from deep inside the womb of the Caribbean Sea. The soft dawn horizontal rays shone behind the ship, projecting its shadow over the water. Many servicemen were already on deck for the morning workout when they heard the warning voice.

"There is an approaching boat."

The deck was soon overflowing with servicemen shooting inquisitive and curious looks at the enigmatic paddler. It was March, 1917, the spring when the United States entered the First European War of the 20th Century, and there were rumors about German submarines in the Caribbean.

The *Memphis* docked in November, 1916, with the first U.S. military occupation of the Dominican Republic. Its captain stared at the boat, trying to decipher the intentions of the baffling paddler that seemed to be alone. He knew the reports about the alleged German presence in those waters, but that didn't bother him.

He had other worries.

What surfaced on his mind was the first American casualty of the occupation, in San Pedro de Macorís, about 45 miles east of Santo Domingo. A kind of suicidal Dominican patriot went up to the U.S. soldiers and started shooting his gun, killing an officer and injuring many servicemen.

The attack wasn't an isolated case.

Gregorio Urbano Gilbert, the patriot, was part of a resistance army that was sprouting in the eastern part of the country. The Americans called them Gavilleros, or at least, in Spanish it sounded like that. Perhaps they did not know the word Guerrilleros, but that is what they were referring to; this was maybe the beginning of the guerrilla warfare resistance in Latin America.

The U.S. Navy knew little about guerrillas. It was 1916, and they had proven unable to catch Pancho Villa in México. They were yet to fight Augusto César Sandino, who rebelled in the Nicaraguan mountains in 1927. Gilbert ended up in Nicaragua as Sandino's secretary. They all fought the same enemy with a different kind of warfare, based on surprise attacks and suicidal ambushes.

They were very dangerous fellows.

The *Memphis*' commander's worries were well founded. He was already concerned about Dominican politicians in Santo Domingo. Their disagreements were taken, at least in part, as an excuse for the military occupation, but now they were stirring up the population's patriotism against the soldiers. In the city everything was fine since the *Memphis* anchored, but that didn't guarantee anything. In war, the captain knew, quiet time just means that the enemy is preparing to launch new attacks.

A strange bond was blooming between some of the occupied city dwellers and many American servicemen. A curious form of affection grew between them, like the kinship among prisoners and jailers, between hostages and kidnappers. The captain, who never trusted that relationship, took his binoculars and confirmed that just one man was in the approaching boat.

"Each man to his post," he ordered, creating all the anticipation that caution recommends.

Many men could be hiding in the boat, or it could be loaded with explosives, making it a floating bomb. Or was it a simple distraction to launch an attack on a different side? There was no fear in the captain, but he had a strong feeling that his mission in Santo Domingo was about to change.

The Surprise

The visitor advanced, facing the sun.

All the light of the new day was shining straight over him

and his small boat. He let the rushing current of the Río Ozama drag the boat down into the Caribbean Sea.

From the approaching boat, the warship seemed like a giant dark vessel lying on the surface. The boat crossed the ría, that green and bluish water border where the river surrenders and the sea swallows it. There, where the Ozama ends and the Caribbean Sea starts, was also the beginning of the *Memphis*' shadow, which the approaching boat slowly penetrated, pulling up next to the warship. Two servicemen jumped down, hand-searched the visitor, inspected the boat, then allowed him on board. As he got closer, the captain observed a strange sense of calmness on the visitor's face. He looked as quiet and determined as those who act moved by deep convictions, who attend the call of duty.

This Dominican patriot did the unthinkable.

Alone and unarmed, he put his own life on the line to surprise the almost 700 men in the *Memphis*' crew. The captain's instinct was correct. The unknown and enigmatic paddler changed forever his mission in Santo Domingo. Never before, or after this event, had any military invaders ever received such a response from the invaded people.

The patriot challenged the occupants to a game of baseball. Just as the Ancient Greeks who celebrated the first Olympic Games, Dominicans used sports instead of war to ventilate political differences. They played with the enemy instead of fighting him. Knowing that a military victory was an illusion, the Dominicans decided to share the things they had in common with the troops and forget those that divided them.

Day after day, invaders and invaded were tied up in endless baseball games and doubleheaders. From there, many things were born. Friendships, fans, female fans, girlfriends and, of course, some babies.

The love for baseball allowed Dominicans and Americans to find something good, a common ground in the stormy political drama they endured. For Dominicans, besides the joy of the game, to beat Americans on the ball field was the only victory they could aspire to. For the Americans, enjoying the game kept them away from the U.S., where an epidemic infectious disease, the so-called

Spanish Flu, was killing thousands. They played and developed new friendships that would end up being far more important than they could have ever imagined.

What happened next summer was natural for Dominicans, but caught the Americans off base. And offguard. On August 31, a hurricane stormed the island's south coast, ripping the *Memphis* to pieces. The stormy waves blasted the vessel against the rocky shore, turning it into a huge box of loose toothpicks floating in the turbulent sea. Around 30 servicemen drowned, but there were far fewer casualties because Dominican fans and ballplayers dove into the troubled waters, rescuing injured and drowning servicemen. They were not an invading army anymore, they were fellow ballplayers. They were friends.

Baseball saved their lives.

Baseball turned what was supposed to be a war of occupation into a friendly encounter. The love of the game overcame the hate of the war, creating an environment where occupants and occupied connected on a deep human level. Facing each other every day in a match of honor, with no other weapon but bats and balls, fostered the awakening of respect and admiration among them.

How did Dominicans become such baseball lovers and players? The game was passed on to them by their Cuban neighbors. Refugees from the The Ten Years War in Cuba, between 1868 and 1878, took two basic things with them, the industrialization of sugar production, and baseball. Many Dominican ballplayers come from sugarcane plantations. It was through those places that the game first entered the country.

Dominicans were grateful for the gift of sugar industrialization and baseball. As if paying for the Cuban generosity, Máximo Gómez, a Dominican military officer from the city of Baní, led the Cuban War of Independence in 1890. This conflict was interrupted by the Cuban U.S.-Spanish War. It lasted 90 days and ended with the Paris Treaty of 1898. Spain ceded to the U.S. Cuba, Puerto Rico and the Philippines.

It was in Cuba, at the end of the 19th Century, that the United States defeated Spain and established itself as the new world imperial power.

While the American troops stationed in Santo Domingo spent time playing ball, others fought the Gavilleros throughout the island. Between games and ambushes, the occupation lasted eight years. The troops retired in 1924, but American businessmen kept the sugar factories built by the Cubans.

The First (and Best) Dominican Ball Player

The American troops left, and one of their best trained military disciples, Rafael Leonidas Trujillo, grabbed power, installing a dictatorship that lasted 30 long years. As a means of pleasing his American masters and gaining the heart of Dominicans, Trujillo's regime fostered the expansion of baseball.

He turned the sport into a political tool.

During the Trujillo Era, between 1930 and 1961, professional baseball teams were founded and the big stadiums that stand today were built across the country. Trujillo, of course, was considered "*The First (and Best) Dominican Ballplayer.*"

Trujillo's older son, Ramfis, was four years old when his father appointed him Air Force Colonel; and he did "*such a good job,*" that by age nine, he was promoted to general. During his successful life, never did he learn to lose, nor had he any intentions of savoring the bitter-sour taste of defeat. That was why he took the two ball teams in Santo Domingo and blended them into a third unbeatable one: Ciudad Trujillo *(Trujillo's City)*. Ramfis, more than a fan, was a baseball addict.

Trujillo's name could have never been linked with losers. If that team was to lose, for any reason, it would have ruined the dictator's political standing.

The 1937 Dominican Baseball Championship was played, "*In support of the Re-election of Presidente Trujillo,*" and, strangely enough, the team with the dictator's name won. The managers took no chances. They got the best players from Cuba and Puerto Rico, then they came recruiting to the United States and went back to the Dominican Republic with players including Leroy "*Satchel*" Paige, one of the best pitchers of all times, Josh Gibson and other superstars of the Negro Leagues. They invested a fortune in foreign players and, in the end, there were more foreigners than Dominicans on the field defending the colors of the dictator's team.

And his "good name."

The umpires supported the Ciudad Trujillo team. The managers knew it. The fans knew it. But that wasn't enough of a guarantee, because losing wasn't a risk worth taking. They involved Trujillo's repressive services in ensuring the championship. The police arrested the managers of the opposing clubs, under charges of "*conspiracy*," to defeat the dictator's team. The best players of those teams were also arrested before their team played Ciudad Trujillo and released after the game was over.

While not on the fields, the American players were subjected to constant surveillance to prevent them from getting drunk or lost in orgies. In reality, they were prisoners, though no one called them that. For the Trujillistas, only a political enemy of the regime would plot to beat the Ciudad Trujillo team in a championship orchestrated to promote President Trujillo's re-election.

In 1937, baseball was subjected to a great deal of political manipulation, but it wasn't the only victim of the dictatorship. That year one of the darkest chapters of Dominican history was written. In a sick mix of racism and nationalism, Trujillo gave the order and over 25,000 Haitian immigrant men, women and children were slaughtered, the majority of them chopped with machetes. That year, Dominican Professional Baseball died too.

Until then, baseball was restricted to the Dominican elite. But it disappeared from that social group and traveled down the social pyramid, deep down, to find its people; the poor.

The sport started a slow, firm and silent recovery, not only in the Dominican Republic, but in other Latin American countries.

In 1937, Orlando —Peruchín— Cepeda was born in Ponce, Puerto Rico. In 1938, Juan Marichal was born in Laguna Verde, in the Dominican province of Montecristi.

That same year, the Argentinean Buck Cannel was narrating the first of the 42 World Series he narrated throughout his career, for Latin American fans.

Between 1938 and 1941, Manuel Mota, Felipe Rojas Alou, Mateo Rojas Alou and Ricardo Carty were born. The same spirit of baseball that united people divided by war, racism, and other social pathologies was readying to perform miracles in the Dominican Republic.

2nd Inning

Top of the Second

A Female Saint Fell From the Heavens

More than a half a century later, as Sammy was breaking homerun records, a plane crash with profound impact on baseball history will long be forgotten. It happened one afternoon in the spring of 1947 in Consuelo, Dominican Republic, Ana Rosa Santoni de Kilbourne's small plane started plunging to the ground.

"We are falling, Señora!" said the pilot, with a broken voice and a strong Cuban accent, stating the obvious to the only passenger of the two engine Beechcraft taking a nose-dive.

That would be the last landing of the most powerful woman for many, many miles around. She looked down, taking a final quick sight of her vast domain and wealth that were proving useless in that decisive moment of her life.

A huge cane field extended farther than her eyes could see, even from above. The snake-like road dug up from the cane fields ran north to south. In the middle of the plantation, almost a mile west of the road, there was a factory where the cane is turned into sugar.

In fractions of a second, a movie-like picture of the most important events of her life crossed Ana Rosa's mind. She was overtaken by fear. She laid back her head, and from her sea-green eyes, two tears slipped down high cheeks, into her ears. She heard the sound of the plane's fuselage hitting the cane field and was convinced that would be the last sound she would ever hear.

It was a few minutes after noon, and the sun was still moving out of its zenith. She looked down again, but didn't see the shadow of the plane, and assumed herself dead, she didn't produce a shadow anymore.

She had become a shadow.

In silence, she prayed and made many promises.

Then she didn't hear, see or feel anything. Her senses were disconnected. She was engulfed in a deep, dark silence that penetrated the emptiness. The Nothingness? Eternity?

Ana Rosa boarded her plane filled with passion for life, as a common mortal, but now she entered another dimension. She stopped being human, and entered the realm of sainthood.

Some of her employees rescued her mortal body from the cane field and, with ritual ceremonial care, as in a sacred procession, they took her home. There she had always been worshiped as a Goddess. Her palace was protected by a brick wall three feet thick by ten feet high. Inside, a Spanish gardener made sure there were always roses, carnations, lillies, and other tropical flowers blooming. A Chinese cook fed the family, and a French steward managed the estate. From Consuelo, she and her husband, the American Edwin Kilbourne, managed many sugar factories in and outside the country.

Ana Rosa recovered from her panic attack, the only thing she suffered in the accident, and ordered an area cleared in the wild, where her cows pastured close to the snaky road. When the plane was crashing she had promised to build a church if she were spared, and she kept her promise. She built a cozy little church, simple and beautiful, with a small choir area made of mahogany wood, with the altar facing the south, the direction of the sea.

She named it "Parroquia Santa Ana", "Saint Ana's Parish." Ana Rosa, now elevated to sainthood, fell from the heavens ten years after the 1937 championship that supported the re-election of President Trujillo. Her "Parroquia Santa Ana" brought about new needs. Even though she was the Santa Patrona, she did not know how, nor was she permitted, to officiate at Mass. This is in addition to the fact that saints do not worship themselves.

That is the duty of mortals.

She needed a priest to provide spiritual guidance to the congregation whose material life was under the total control of this new living saint and her American husband. Most of the people in the area surrounding their sugar factory made a living tied to the sugar business, either as employees, or providing services to those employees. The two controlled everything, including the union that represented their workers. Now they were setting out to control the community's spiritual life.

After changing owners many times, from Cubans to Americans, the plantation formerly known as Ingenio Agua Dulce, now Ingenio Consuelo, ended up in the hands of this Cuban-American couple. Their prosperity turned Consuelo into an attractive immigrant destination. People from all over the Caribbean, the British, French and Dutch colonies ended up there, in addition to the neighboring Haitians.

Way back when, years before modern sociologists invented multiculturalism as a concept, Consuelo was a multicultural center, but the people were so poor they did not know that. At the time when Ana Rosa's plane crashed, English, French, Dutch and, of course, Spanish, were spoken in Consuelo.

The immigrant group that had the most active participation in the community life came from the British colonies, and were called Cocolos. They had many advantages over other immigrant groups and the natives themselves. They arrived in Consuelo as experienced industrial workers, and Dominicans had no industrial experience. Their native language was English, another big advantage in this Spanish speaking country. The Cocolos could speak the language of the Americans, who were the new plantation owners. Since Dominicans only spoke Spanish, they couldn't communicate with the Americans.

The company offered some benefits for its executives, including free, decent housing, and education for their children, at "Escuela Evelyn," named after Ana Rosa and Mr. Kilbourne's daughter. The company also had a baseball team, where its executives, their sons, and a few others could play, by invitation only. In Consuelo, baseball was still an elite sport. The working poor, the immigrants from Haiti and the British colonies, or their families, did not participate in the game. They were only accepted as fans.

The Resurrection

In 1947, many important things happened in baseball.

On April 15th, Jackie Robinson became the first black player in the white Major Leagues. He broke the racial divide in baseball, speeding up the process that ended racial segregation not only in the sport but eventually throughout most of American society. That year, a miracle occurred in a peasant community in northwestern Dominican Republic. A little boy was sleeping in a coma for over a week. His relatives gathered around his bed waiting for him to exhale his last breath. A week earlier, he suffered a cramp while swimming, and he almost drowned, but was fished out of the pond, and now he lay motionless.

The doctor said that if he didn't awake in seven days he would die. It was 11:45 PM of his seventh day in bed.

In slow motion, the child moved his left foot first.

Then lifted his leg little by little until he had it almost in a vertical position. Juan Antonio Marichal Sánchez returned from the dead, lifting the very foot that would later become his trademark as one of the most famous pitchers in the world.

In 1947 the Second European War was the center of the world's attention, and no one noticed two important things in the history of world baseball: Juan Marichal's resurrection, and Ana Rosa's plane crash.

The Saint and Her Priest

The search for a priest for the Parroquia Santa Ana went as far as Canada, where Father Joseph Ainslie was hired. He was a young and handsome priest with liberal ideas.

The community translated his name into Spanish, calling him Padre José.

When Padre José arrived, Consuelo was a shantytown, formed by a handful of old houses built with discarded material from the sugar factory. There were no toilets, no schools nor hospitals, not even drinking water, except at a public faucet. The only abundant commodity in Consuelo was poverty, but the people were so poor they did not even have the necessary knowledge to figure out their poverty.

Padre José found a nonexistent congregation.

Those who were supposed to be his flock were corroded by misery and injustice. Their lives were controlled by a bunch of moneylenders dressed up as union leaders. Before he could "cure" their spirits and souls, he needed to rescue their bodies from social injustice.

His outrage began with his first Mass. He had low tolerance for the high level of injustice flourishing in his new parish. There were people standing up for lack of seats, but the first three pews on the right side of the church were empty. No one dared to sit in them. They were the "private seats" of Santa Ana Rosa and her close aides. Padre José saw this as a clear and offensive privilege "inside" the House of God, but he did not protest the situation. After all, it was Ana Rosa's church.

Outside church, matters were even worse.

The Kilbournes knew that they did not pay enough money so that their workers could buy themselves home clocks or wristwatches to be on time for work every day. That is why they instituted a special kind of public clock. The sharp whistle of a siren reminded the entire village of the time to start work. From then on, this whistle controlled Consuelo's life. Even today, that community lives from whistle to whistle.

Every morning the indecent whistle woke up even the roosters. When padre José landed in Consuelo, there were two daily shifts of 12 hours, and an equal number of whistles. The fortunate ones who had a job, worked for six months of the year and earned $1.30 per day, it was a little more than a dime an hour. By then the U.S. dollar was legal currency in the Dominican Republic.

To get a job, people needed to wait until their name came up on the list, and when that happened, their "union" gave them a $10 loan, whether they asked for it or not. Every Saturday the company withheld $2 in weekly interest for the union's loan. It was a unique rate, 20 percent per week, 80 per cent a month. The yearly interest rate was 1,040 per cent.

This reality called for action.

Padre José needed to perform a very unusual ceremony: exorcise the many demons living within the body of his congregation and in the whole community. That was the only way in which he could ever have a congregation of his own. His mission was clear, but he had no experience, nor did he know the prayer and liturgy needed to exorcise those demons.

A few weeks after his arrival, and trying to avoid going crazy, he did something very stupid. He jumped in his jeep, bought by Mr. Kilbourne, and drove quickly through the streets. A dust cloud chased him and caught up to him when he stopped the vehicle across from the only park in the village.

It was Saturday, payday. Workers and moneylenders were around the park waiting for their money. When he got there, he took out a loudspeaker and called the workers to rise up demanding better wages and working conditions. He told them that Mr. Kilbourne's horses lived better than they did, and that they had the right and the duty to protest against this situation.

The workers' reaction to his speech was simple: They walked away and left Padre José alone. Without an audience, he started his jeep and went back to the church house. He stopped the jeep without turning off the engine, went in and came out with some personal items in his hand, put them in the jeep and took off again.

He stopped before entering the main road that ran close to the church, waiting for other cars to pass. While waiting, he saw the Arab merchants and the prostitutes getting ready to leave after offering their products and services to the workers, as they did every payday. The afternoon was dying out, the dark and silent curtain of the night was falling over Consuelo. When he got a chance, he stepped on the accelerator and disappeared into the cane fields, followed by the sound of the engine, his fading taillights twinkling like distant fireflies in the darkness of the early evening.

Padre José ran away. He went to spend the night elsewhere, deeper into the plantation, to recover from his defeat. The following day, even if no parishioner would show up, he still had to celebrate Sunday Mass. When morning broke, he was back at his church, but he was not surprised to see that Ana Rosa's private pews were empty, and few parishioners showed up. That Sunday only the most faithful and courageous church members attended the service. More than a worship service, they had an informal conversation. The congregation was interested in saving their souls and keeping their jobs, but that seemed to be somewhat difficult at the time; they needed to choose between their church and their job and they made a clear selection.

A war was declared.

Mr. Kilbourne, the lord and owner of cane fields and all forms of life within them, despised the young and rebellious priest. The executives of his company also hated him out of obedience and loyalty to their boss. Some of them felt an inexplicable envy at the place the young, handsome, muscular and rebellious Padre José occupied in the fantasies of their own wives.

Many women used to go, against their husbands' wishes, to assist in cleaning the priest's living quarters. They kept their secret hope of becoming the Serpent of Paradise that would tempt Padre José to break his vow of celibacy.

The young priest's life was threatened by two basic dangers: the hate from the company's executives and the desire of some of their wives. To defend his life and his celibacy while fighting the Santa was his immediate destiny.

The war between the Santa and her priest had just begun.

Baseball has proven to be the best medicine against poverty for many people who were born among the cane fields.

Archivos Dominicanos

The Collective Exorcism

Sitting on the stairs of his deserted church, Padre José was depressed after losing his first battle. Kidnapped by desolation, his sight was lost in the cane fields, when something caught his attention.

Dozens of people across the street from the church were cheering and screaming in a loud and happy way. They were having a very good time and he thought they were celebrating the death of his ministry, but he was wrong.

He stood up and walked toward the group.

Barefoot, with pieces of tree branches, a ball made out of an old sock, and without gloves, the workers and their children were playing baseball.

Never had he seen so much happiness in that place.

And he read the scene as a message from Jesus Christ. Baseball would help him organize the community and conduct the necessary collective exorcism to save his ministry.

He became involved with the group and proposed to organize a team. The idea was well received and the congregation baptized their club with the name of their parish Santa Ana. That was Consuelo's first community organization.

The love for baseball defeated their fear of losing their jobs, and they worked with the priest by means of the team. He organized the community using teamwork technique, just as in the baseball team, to achieve collective goals.

Basic rules of the game applied to community life. Sacrifice and cooperation were among the most important ones. Baseball players, unless they are home run hitters like Sammy Sosa, are unable to score a run if others don't bat them in; to bat in a run, someone needs to be on base. The players learned to sacrifice their individual turns at bat, to move ahead the winning run.

From the pulpit, Padre José talked about Christ's individual sacrifice to save humanity. With this blend of baseball and religion, the young priest achieved his goal: he organized the community.

The philosophy of individual sacrifice in the name of collective welfare was their inspiration. The workers risked their jobs in the name of their community and it paid off. The church was always filled with youth, and Parroquia Santa Ana became a place where there were always parishioners.

Baseball and more openness in the church saved Padre José's ministry.

With baseball the people from Consuelo learned to take care of themselves. Every player contributed a few pennies to purchase sports gear. The whole community worked to prepare the diamond. The fever not only took over the young men, but their mothers and sisters also participated. It was Doña Alicia Guerrero who sewed the uniforms. She was the mother of one of the country's most outstanding stand up comedians, Tirso Guerrero, known also as the Negro Plebe. Other women prepared meals for the players of visiting teams that came to play Santa Ana. A spirit of cooperation took over the community in a few month's times. The priest then founded a cooperative and a credit union to compete with the moneylenders, the union leaders loyal to Mr. Kilbourne.

The baseball team could not be discredited because it bore the name of the Santa Patrona and, together with the credit union, demonstrated that the community, once united, could attain any goal. Then Padre José expanded the scope of his activism, aiming at a very big objective.

When the community was organized around the Parroquia Santa Ana, the baseball team, and the credit union, they started asking for more benefits. They started fighting for a housing program and eight-hour work shifts.

The Big Battle

Two things benefited the community.

The first was Trujillo's interest in Mr. Kilbourne's property. This was the reason why he did not repress the labor movement. It allowed the community, already united, to press the American businessman against the wall.

One afternoon Padre José made a smart move.

He used the baseball team and summoned the workers to a unusual rally, with such strange speakers as a blind immigrant and a union leader. One of them was the country's blind Catholic bishop, Monseñor Ricardo Pitini. An Italian immigrant, Pitini was the old fox of the clergy. He delivered a political speech wrapped up in a christian sermon, standing on the steps of the bridge from where the factory's railroads were controlled. He talked about saving the soul while taking care of the body's needs.

Padre José had briefed him about the situation and the bishop launched an indirect but powerful attack against the moneylenders acting as union leaders. He told the workers that since he, Pitini, was blind, he could not do it himself, but he recommended they keep an eye on the union's treasurer: ojo con el tesorero, he shouted in Spanish, while pointing at his blind eyes with his index finger.

The expression became a slogan for the upcoming battles.

The next speaker was a tall, strong man with dark skin and a thunderous, incendiary voice, named Mauricio Báez. He defended the workers' rights to decent wages, eight-hour shifts, housing, health care programs and education for their children. That was the last public appearance of this man, by then the most important union leader in the country. After that, he had to go underground and flee to Cuba, where later Trujillo's henchmen killed him.

The community unity at the rally was a hard blow to the company. Without government support, with the church and the workers against him, Mr. Kilbourne was cornered and ready to surrender, but he did not give up without a fight. He tried to scare the people by firing many workers.

The Cocolos were his first victims.

This human group was not Catholic, but they became the strongest supporters of Padre José and his community activism. Many of the fired workers ended up at other sugar factories in the area, such as Santa Fe, Porvenir and Quisqueya. The firing scared no one, for they were all willing to let go of their jobs before breaking the unity of the community. Mr. Kilbourne then changed his tactic and offered them housing. He built barracks to house multiple families. Padre José said that not even a horse could live decently in them, and they were rejected. As Mr. Kilbourne was giving in, the community put more pressure on him.

They demanded individual houses.

Against his will, Mr. Kilbourne ordered a model house built, and called representatives of the community organizations to inspect it. Delegates from the baseball team Parroquia Santa Ana, from the credit union, and from the church itself met in the church to evaluate the offer. Each house had two bedrooms, a living room, kitchen, and a bathroom with a shower.

The yard was large enough to have pigs, goats and chickens, it also had land enough to grow a vegetable garden. That enabled the workers to survive the Tiempo Muerto *(dead time)* which was the six months with no sugar production and no work. Each family would have a vital and private space much larger than they had anticipated; many houses were in such a big lot that they could have a baseball diamond in the yard.

The community shared other things besides baseball.

The houses did not have indoor toilets and, at a strategic point between every six yards or so, there was a multifamily latrine with half a dozen private cubicles.

The community leaders put their seal of approval on the model house, and Mr. Kilbourne ordered a rush on the construction. Bulldozers and other heavy equipment opened roads into the woods as quickly as they could. The result was that many streets ended up spreading out in a fork-like way, creating unconventional corners.

Whomever stops today at one of these corners, where the streets converge but do not intersect, might think they are in the batter's box at home plate. The streets have such a curious layout that one who decided to run down a street to the right, as if to first base, can keep on going around and get back to their departure point running from the left side.

Many streets fan out like this, making Consuelo look like a collection of baseball diamonds. With this strange design, three barrios were built. The first got a very objective name: Pueblo Nuevo, which means "New Town." The others are Guachupita and La Habana.

The families who were living in little shanty huts were relocated to new and clean houses. Padre José then asked the construction company that built the new housing units, to remove the old huts and build a baseball diamond in their place. Thanks to baseball, Consuelo is the only sugar estate in the Dominican Republic with individual houses for the workers.

But their improved new housing was not the only community achievement. The daily work shift was set at eight hours, even though it did not become law until 1951 under Trujillo's Labor Act.

Many years later, Trujillo, having consolidated his power, paid one of the eternal debts that poor countries always owe the United States. In the name of that debt, the American government controlled Dominican's customs service as a way of collecting their monthly payments. After the pay off, Trujillo recovered the customs and created the Dominican monetary system.

The U.S. dollar had been the country's legal currency until that point. The dictator also activated his contacts in the Catholic Church. He considered Padre José a dangerous Communist threat and managed to deport him back to Canada.

This Canadian priest, in silence, without public notice, wrote one of the most glorious pages in the history of the Latin American Roman Catholic Church. It was one of those few occasions that did justice to the name Catholic, which means universal. Padre José opened the doors of his church to those with other Christian affiliations. His church was filled with Anglican, Pentecostal and other Protestant groups, because the Cocolos, who were the majority of the industrial workers, were not Roman Catholics. Padre José created an environment in which Catholics and Protestants united on the basis of their Christian faith, the love of baseball and the will to fight for their community.

The young priest was part of a new movement in the church that assumed the fight for social justice as an essential part of their Christian duty. Other priests would later react against injustice, even if they were not as successful. After Padre José, came *"Liberation Theology"* and the guerrilla priests. In February 1965, outraged by social in-justice, Camilo Torres, a Roman Catholic priest, united the gun and the gospel in the Colombian mountains, and died fighting in guerrilla warfare.

After Padre José was no longer in Consuelo or even in the country, after Trujillo "cleared" the place of that "communist," he also cleared it of Mr. Kilbourne. The dictator took over Consuelo, and the entire sugar industry in the country.

One afternoon he was on his way to Higüey, a town in the far eastern end of the island, to attend a religious ceremony in the Basilica de la Virgen de la Altagracia, Trujillo passed through Consuelo, and saw many men of all ages playing baseball. That made him angry. He thought they should be working instead of playing. He ordered the baseball diamond destroyed and turned it into a cane field.

Austin Jacobo, one of the community activists from Padre José's movement, protested the official decision. He complained that the community fought hard to get their baseball diamond from an American, and now it was paradoxically going to be destroyed by a Dominican. His protest almost cost him his life; he was forced to flee Consuelo. He moved to The Bronx, New York, where he died doing community activism.

Lazy Boys!

A mi me llaman el negrito del batey
porque el trabajo para mi es un enemigo
el trabajar yo se lo dejo todo al buey
porque el trabajo lo hizo Dios como un castigo.

I am called the little black guy from the batey
because I consider work my enemy;
I leave all work to the ox,
because work was made by God as a punishment,

So goes a famous merengue song.

That point of view was shared by many people.

"This is not for me, this is for animals," shouted an arrogant teenager before throwing the ax with which he was cutting logs, rejecting a job that could carry him to one of Consuelo's best executive positions. He was privileged, but like so many other adolescents, he did not understand that. He was so focused on himself that he only knew his hands hurt, he had blisters all over them, and had sweated almost to the point of dehydration during the first hours of his shift.

His comments hurt his uncle's feelings and sense of pride, since he did that same work, without considering himself an animal. His uncle was trying to teach him the secrets and crafts of the job and, offended, he hit him with a saw, before the young man ran away.

This was a family feud.

The teenager was the grandson of Gaston, a Cocolo who migrated from the island of Saint Marteen and spoke English, French, Dutch and Spanish. He was something like a mayor in Consuelo. He ran a working crew that clea ned the village. His basic duty was logging to feed the factory boilers. From those boilers the factory got its power to keep the mill grinding cane. Its steam fed the whistle that controlled life in Consuelo.

The brothers, male children and grandchildren of Gaston worked as his assistants. The males in the family learned the job to make sure one of them inherited it. That teenager, however, had no interest whatsoever in working or going to school. He spent all his time with other boys who, just as lazy as himself, were obsessed with baseball.

When he abandoned the ax and ran away, Ricardo Carty was entering uncertainty. He started walking a non-existent path and, as the poet Antonio Machado said, "he made a path as he walked." He took the road not yet traveled, got away from Consuelo, and certainly farther than he could have gone with the ax.

Many others would follow his example.

Life is extremely hard, bitter and sour for the workers who make sugar for a living.

Archivos Dominicanos

3rd Inning

Top of the Third

The Midwife

That Tuesday Oliva, Gaston's daughter and Polo's wife, left her house in Guachupita to take care of an emergency call. In her right hand she carried a mahogany wood briefcase that looked like an extension of her long-stylized dark arm. In it she carried the tools of her trade. She was Consuelo's midwife on her way to the house of a woman in labor.

She passed by a big Centenary Ceiba tree. Its roots rose out of the ground, extending as arms and legs, and its trunk shaped as a mythological giant. Many ghost tales are woven around that tree, planted at the corner of Oliva's house.

We pass the comb, she read on a rustic sign painted on a piece of cardboard, advertising a hot comb for hairdressing. It was the beginning of what may have been Consuelo's beauty salon service industry. Oliva continued on her way, passing under a flamboyant tree that, for that time of the year, seemed as though dressed up for a party, filled with red and yellow flowers in brilliant colors.

We sell ice and ice cream, she read on another sign.

She ascended a small rocky hill and passed in front of another house with a sign that brought her back to an old family worry.

We give shots, the other sign said.

There she remembered her son Ricardo.

He didn't want to work or study and spent all his time at the river and on the baseball diamond. Since Padre José arrived in Consuelo, the people's lives improved, but that was only part of the truth. The rest of it was that many young men lost interest in working and fell madly in love with a game. Oliva once took Ricardo to the hospital where she worked as a nurse. She harbored the secret hope that when the boy saw the doctors working, he would be interested in health care and become the doctor she could not be.

The lad, however, did not pay attention to anything; he seemed to be a lazy boy with strong convictions about his laziness; he refused to grow up, he only wanted to play. Oliva was so absorbed in her thoughts that she crossed the barrio La Habana and the public market of the village without even noticing them. She arrived at her destination.

The woman in labor lived in one of the first barracks built by Mr. Kilbourne. It was a sample home that was rejected by the community because Padre José said not even a horse could live in them with dignity.

He was right.

Inside the barracks, the hallway served as a collective kitchen. When Oliva arrived, she saw a table next to a wall with a hot plate for each resident. On one of them there was a pot of boiling water. That indicated to her where the pregnant woman was.

The rooms of these barracks could be filled by a small bed. The residents could not lie down. They had to dive in the bed from the door because, inside the room, there was not enough space to walk. They were as small as the bathroom in a cheap apartment. Oliva entered sideways, with her back against the wall, facing the bed, over which she opened her briefcase and took out scissors, forceps and other instruments.

The woman who was about to deliver knew what she needed to do because this was not her first child. She made herself comfortable, opened her legs and Oliva received the newborn. Then she cut the umbilical cord, lifted the baby boy by the ankles with the head down and spanked him. The scream announced that his lungs started to function. She cleaned and checked the baby over before passing him to his mother, who immediately cuddled him.

It was August the 23, 1958, when Ricardo Carty's mother, acting as Doña Cuta's midwife, delivered Julio César Franco. New promises for baseball were being born, but no one noticed. That year, Puerto Rican Peruchin Cepeda was elected Rookie of the Year in the National League, Felipe

Rojas Alou moved up to the Major Leagues and Venezuelan Luis Aparicio became the first Latin American player to win a Golden Glove Award.

The following year, on January the first, an unknown, bad and unfit Cuban amateur pitcher amazed the whole world. Fidel Castro had long since given up his baseball dreams when he came down from the Sierra Maestra to change forever the political map of the Americas.

The Cuban Revolution had triumphed.

As a direct consequence, a wave of Cuban immigration flooded South Florida, and today they are the largest Hispanic group in that state.

The 13 Contracts Player

In 1959, the Liga Dominicana de Béisbol Profesional, the Dominican Professional Baseball League, was founded and became affiliated with organized baseball in the United States. That step institutionalized the sport and opened up a road for Dominicans to play with American teams. Since then, American baseball teams have sent their rookie players to expand their training during the Dominican winter baseball season. In the Dominican Republic, the professional baseball season runs from November to February. From April on, Dominican fans follow the American Major Leagues.

In 1959, the Dominican Republic attempted again to win the Pan-American Amateur Baseball Championship held in Chicago. Felipe Rojas Alou and Julián Javier led the Dominican team to win that championship in Mexico during the summer of 1955, and they caught the attention of the American scouts. The following year, Felipe came to the United States for the first time to play baseball, and Osvaldo *–El Orégano–* Virgil became the first Dominican to play in the Majors. That year, Luis Aparicio was the first Latin American chosen as Rookie of the Year.

During the first game of the 1959 championship, and with his second turn at bat, Ricardo Carty hit a home run, sending the ball into the bleachers between left and center field in Comiskey Park. In the second half of that inning, another ball skyrocketed and was headed out of the park when Carty leapt and caught it. Leaning against the wall, he threw the ball to home plate and put out the runner trying to score.

The fans went crazy.

The Major League scouts were obsessed with Carty's performance, and, at the end of the championship, something very curious happened. Scouts from nine American teams formed an organized line to ask Mr. Carty to play with them. They offered him the opportunity to do what he wanted most in life: to play baseball. To do so, he only needed to sign a piece of paper.

It seemed like a pretty good deal to him.

The more contracts he signed, the more opportunities he would have to play. Or so he thought. But in the end, nine American teams and four from the Dominican Republic had contracts signed by Carty. He signed with 13 teams in just a few hours. Afterward, the nine American teams went to court, fighting for the right to have the son of Consuelo's midwife play with them. Because of signing with so many teams, Carty almost ended up banned forever from playing baseball in the U.S. However, since he did not take money from anyone, the court declared all the contracts invalid.

"They were telling me, 'sign here to play with us,' and I signed; I only wanted to play ball. Some offered to pay me a bonus but I rejected all money offers; I did not want money, I only wanted to play," said Carty during an interview while driving his car through the streets of San Pedro de Macorís.

In the Dominican Republic, there were other problems.

One of the teams for which Carty had signed, the Leones del Escogido, was sponsored by the Trujillo family. Another one, Las Estrellas Orientales from San Pedro de Macorís, was lead by Rafael Antún one of Trujillo's many compadres *(which is ritual kinship between parents and godparents)*. The compadres fought for Carty and Antun won, arguing that the player should stay with his hometown team, Estrellas Orientales.

That same year in Los Cuatro Caminos *(the Four Roads)*, one of San Pedro's barrios, Jorge Bell was born, and in Los

Angeles, Ecuadorian Jaime Jarrín started his career as a sportscaster, narrating the L.A. Dodgers games in Spanish.

The following spring, Carty flew to Davenport, Iowa, to report to the training camp of the Milwaukee Braves. Also in 1959, Rudy Hernández, Julián Javier, Juan Marichal, Guayubín Olivo, and Mateo Rojas Alou all moved up to the Majors.

In the beginning of the 60's, Dominican players started to build a reputation of their own in Major League Baseball.

The Sower

Ricardo *—Rico— (which means "rich" just as in English)—* Carty returned to Consuelo every year. He drove a huge Pontiac Bonneville, the most beautiful and glamorous car in the whole batey and beyond. Driving it slowly through the dusty and rocky streets and into the narrowest alleys, he gave away balls, gloves and bats. It seems as if he spent his free time in the United States picking up used sports equipment to bring back with him to Consuelo.

He gave away gloves, balls, bats and all the equipment he could get. Carty planted baseballs in every corner of Consuelo.

The harvest season would come years later in the Majors. Hundreds of players were signed in Consuelo, *Pepe* Frías, *El Gallo* Batista, Alfredo Griffin, Nelson Norman and Julio Franco are only a few of the most famous. All, without exception, got a ball from Carty's hands or played with the balls he brought to Consuelo.

By 1963 the fruits of Padre José's grassroots work began to blossom. Carty from the Santa Ana team, a Cocolo from Consuelo, became the 12th Dominican in the Majors.

That same year, Pedro González and Jesús Rojas Alou, two of Carty's countrymen, came to play in the Majors.

During the 60s, the first invasion of Latin American ballplayers descended upon the Majors, 22 of them from the Dominican Republic. Baseball continued to change the lives of poor and humble men, taking them well beyond their most ambitious dreams.

Bottom of the Third

La Fiesta del Chivo

From the back seat of his black 1960 Cadillac, he saw that in the reflection of the headlights, the falling rain drops seemed like tiny phalluses penetrating the darkness. That fed the magic of his pre-sexual encounter. He was on his way to take a dive into the arms and legs of his favorite mistress. Yes, favorite, because he had many. The raindrops hitting the windshield became harder, then turned into the bullets that killed dictator Rafael Leonidas Trujillo that Tuesday night, May 30, 1961.

By then, Roger Maris had only 11 of the 61 home runs with which he broke the record of 60 homers established by Babe Ruth in 1927.

"Mataron al chivo, en la carretera"

"The male goat was killed on the highway" said the popular song with which the dictator's death was celebrated. Trujillo was called el chivo (the male goat), and his death created a huge political crisis. For some, it was a tragedy. For others, it was a reason to celebrate, to party, to make fiesta—la fiesta del chivo.

That was how Dominicans entered the tumultuous decade of the 60s.

Early one Autumn morning in 1962, Pentagon officials entered the bedroom of President John F. Kennedy while he was still sleeping. They woke him and showed him something frightening indeed. Only 90 miles from Florida, Fidel Castro had nuclear missiles pointing toward the U.S. And so began the infamous Crisis de Octubre, as the Cubans call the Missile Crisis. Never before, or since, had the so called *"Cold War"* been so hot, so much so that it almost exploded into a nuclear war.

After the crisis was resolved, the U.S. embargo against

Cuba was tightened, closing the doors of the Major Leagues to Cuban players who chose to live on the island. By the same token, the same doors were opened evern wider for Dominican players. That year, Kennedy was busy with Castro and, in December, Juan Bosch, a Dominican liberal, won the first free elections held after 30 years of Trujillo's dictatorship.

Oh September!

For Dominicans, September 1963, is an unforgettable month. During those 30 days, Jesús Rojas Alou was called to the Majors without knowing he was entering baseball history. The evening of September 10th, at Candlestick Park in San Francisco, his brother Felipe was patrolling right field for the Giants. Willie McCovey was in the left while "Say Hey" Willie Mays was in center. In the sixth inning, the Giants were 13 runs ahead of the New York Mets.

The Giants' manager, Alvin Dark, decided to let some of his new players in the game, allowing the experienced ones to rest. He made baseball history. McCovey, who had hit three home runs in that game, was sent to first base to take it easy. The rookie, Jesús Rojas Alou, was called to fill in for him. Dark sent Mays to rest in the dugout and opened a spot in center field that was filled by Mateo Rojas Alou.

It was September 10th, 1963, when the *"Three Red Devils,"* as the Rojas Alou brothers were called in Dominican baseball, became the only three brothers to play in the same game for the same team in baseball history.

In 1963, Ellis Pérez, Billy Berroa, Max Alvarez, Osvaldo Cepeda y Cepeda and Freddy Mondesi *(Raúl Mondesí's father)* began to narrate baseball games on the Dominican radio waves. The following year, Tony Oliva became the third Latin American chosen Rookie of the Year.

More interesting things were happening in the Dominican Republic. A group of soldiers backed by the Kennedy Administration kicked Juan Bosch out of office. With this military coup, Dominicans discovered that by killing Trujillo, they had not got rid of Trujillism. They killed the dog, but the rabies did not die with him.

Two years later, in April 1965, a group of military officers rebelled against the government and tried to restore constitutional order by bringing Bosch back into office. A Haitian immigrant descendant who had survived the brutal massacre of 1937 took a leading role in the crisis. José Francisco Peña Gómez asked for, and received, popular support for the military rebels that demanded the restoration of Bosch's Constitutional government.

The Dominican Civil War began, but it was set aside to fight another war, a patriotic one. Another Haitian descendant, Colonel Raul Benoit, called for and obtained American support. The Johnson Administration sent 25,000 U.S. soldiers from the 82nd Airborne division to invade the country, stop the rebels and defend the military that had ousted Bosch. These soldiers didn't play baseball as had those at the beginning of the century. In 1965 they played war games. The country was wrapped in bloodshed and poisoned with wrath.

April in Consuelo

Even though the *Revolución de Abril* never left the capital city of Santo Domingo, the people of Consuelo had great participation in the conflict. Early one afternoon, during this second American occupation, a group of boys were playing a quick three inning game in the yard of the sugar mill's horse barn before going to school. Some ran after the ball, while others were scoring runs when a whistle blew, followed by a few silent seconds, then another whistle sounded.

It was 1:30 p.m.; a warning for workers to get ready for the two o'clock shift. Then a P-51 bomber roared in the sky, and the street was filled with people, though not all were going to work.

"*Intelligence reports,*" as public rumors were called in those days, said that the Dominican Air Force, then supporting the Trujillista's military force, was going to bomb a nearby bridge. It is unknown how or why, but someone convinced the people of Consuelo that the bridge was important to them, so important that they decided to risk their lives to defend it.

They formed Commandos as well armed as they could to

defend the bridge. They carried sticks, knives, sharp knives, very sharp knives, more knives, machetes, and slings; one carried a harpoon. They all carried different weapons, but they shared something in common, like a uniform.

Every one of them carried a big mirror.

They took down the mirrors from their homes and brought them to the battle field. The rationale was simple: they were going to put the mirrors up on the bridge and when the pilots tried to see the target before pulling the trigger, they would see only the mirrors reflecting the sun. They would end up blind and crash into the bushes with their infamous planes.

Mirrors were considered the best and most advanced anti-air force technology available. In Consuelo, some families managed to put their big double mirrored wardrobes on their roof tops as protection against possible air attacks. The people from Consuelo had a deep rooted faith in the strategic defensive power of mirrors.

It may have been the mirrors, but the planes came and attacked, not the bridge, but rather Consuelo's Commandos, who were successful in escaping without casualties.

During the 1965 *Revolución de Abril*, the only person who died in Consuelo was the owner of a local brothel. He was found one morning floating in his own blood, and it was never clear what happened or who killed him. There were some suspects arrested, but no one was charged. It was said that an unsatisfied customer stabbed him in a feud over the quality of his services.

The American occupation of 1965 ended a year later, as new immigration laws were approved in the United States, opening the doors to a flood of Dominican immigrants. All the slogans against the soldiers seemed to have boiled down and steamed up to:

"*Yankee Go Home!…and Take Me With You!*"

4th Inning

Top of the Fourth

Do You Want More?

The people of Consuelo, thanks to the sharp whistle, developed an extraordinary and perceptive sense of hearing. Without leaving their homes, they knew about everything important that was going on beyond their batey. Baseball. They could "see" with their fine-tuned ears. With them, they penetrated the thick darkness of the night that enveloped the cane fields, traveled thousands of miles and "saw" all the action in Major League Baseball.

They "saw" that historic moment when Dominicans became famous using their bats in the Majors. It was in a great match controlled by old feuds and new misunderstandings. No one missed that titanic duel in a double-header between the L.A. Dodgers and the San Francisco Giants, at the end of the 1965 season. Both teams had dragged old conflicts from the East to the West coast, since the days when the Dodgers were in Brooklyn and the Giants in The Bronx.

That Sunday, two of the best pitchers in baseball history were fighting to prevail over the mound of San Francisco's Candlestick Park. Sandy Koufax pitched for the Dodgers and Juan Marichal for the Giants.

In the top of the third, Marichal was batting, had one strike, and let the second pitch go by. The Dodgers' catcher, John Roseboro, threw the ball back to Koufax. Without apparent reason, Marichal started walking backward, toward the mound, waving the bat in his hands, and Roseboro followed him.

Everyone in Consuelo "saw" the scene.

Roseboro, with clenched fists and ready to punch, went after Marichal. The sound of a bat was heard. Roserboro's face was flooded with blood. Peruchín Cepeda and Koufax walked closer to them and, in seconds, they were in the middle of a huge crowd of players.

From Consuelo, the fans "saw" every detail of the squabble between them. From Roseboro's left eye down, all his body was covered with blood that kept pouring, like water from a broken pipe. Roseboro kept right on going. Marichal took a few steps back and stood offering him the bloody bat as a threat, asking him: "*¿Quieres más?*" *("Do you want more?")*

Players from both teams, the umpires and the police calmed the situation. And the explanations followed.

Marichal argued that when Roseboro returned the ball to Koufax, he was almost hit in the ear with the ball. He said that the Dodgers' players wanted revenge against him, because of a dead ball he threw to one of the team's sluggers.

Everyone agreed that the American occupation of the Dominican Republic and the internal racial tensions in the U.S. contributed to the fight. Once again, baseball, with a Dominican player included, was in the middle of political games.

By hitting Roseboro with the bat, Marichal established a terrible reputation for himself, for Dominicans, and for Latin American players. Marichal became the new and most hated villain in the United States. The American press printed atrocities about the Monstruo de Laguna Verde *(The Monster of Green Lagoon, as he is known among Dominicans).*

The ball, according to Dominican fans' popular philosophy, is round, but comes in a square box, and therefore no one can count victory until the last out, the 27th. That was also Marichal's number.

His time in the doghouse did not last longer than a human pregnancy. By June 1966, nine months later, nine photos of Marichal appeared on the cover of Time magazine.

"The best right arm in baseball."

That was the headline of the feature story in which it was first said that the Dominican pitcher deserved his own place in the Hall of Fame and at the Smithsonian Institution in Washington DC.

Besides Marichal, at the end of the 1966 season, many

Dominican players made positive impressions in the Majors. When the National League batting championship was decided, this was the result: In first place with a .342 average, Mateo Rojas Alou, second place with a .327 average his brother Felipe and third place at .326, Ricardo Carty. From then on, Dominican players have been respected whenever, and wherever they stand with a bat in their hands. That year, many Latin American stars shone in the Big Show. Puerto Rican Roberto Clemente became the first Latin American chosen as MVP in the National League, and Luis Aparicio won another Golden Glove Award.

In 1966, Juan Bosch returned to the Dominican Republic to participate in a strange "election" organized by the American troops that invaded the country to support the Trujillistas. Joaquín Balaguer, one of Trujillo's puppet presidents, "won" the "election." He presided over a country torn by the wrath of hatred, poisoned with resentments and craving revenge; plenty of people were well armed and decided to continue their interrupted civil war.

Balaguer remained in office for 12 long and difficult years.

They Escaped

When Carty dumped the ax to pick up the bat, he did not know where he was heading. He just knew what he was running away from. The workers in Consuelo worked to support the money lenders or chupa sangre (blood suckers), as they are called. They were the first to get money on payday.

Armed with long sharp knives and unfriendly faces, the money lenders would stand in front of the company's payment office every Saturday. It was payday and they collected the interest on their loans.There were times when workers got away without paying them, creating heated discussions and serious threats of knife fights.

Once upon a Saturday, a moneylender got involved in an extremely stressful discussion with a worker about his uncollected money. He became so incensed that his fat-covered heart suffered a lethal attack. His relatives began looking for the client, first of all, to collect the outstanding debt and interests, as was the will of the deceased, before killing him in revenge.

To avoid these conflicts, the company wisely decided to move ahead at least 40 years into the future. They "privatized" the payment process. All the payroll money was sent to the office of the most important money lender of the batey who, as a "volunteer," distributed the cash. He took his part first, then gave the workers what was left over. Every Saturday there was a line of depressed men pleading for some money in his office. Many were pleading for permission to take a few crumbs of their own hard-earned wages to appease their children's hunger. Others were asking for money to intoxicate themselves with booze and have some fun with the hookers. After all, it was their money; they sweated to earn every penny of it and had the right to spend it however they chose.

The workers who were able to get some cash from the money lenders had to overcome many obstacles before they made it home. The whorehouses far outnumbered the meat and vegetable markets, grocery stores, pharmacies, hardware stores, schools, shoe repair stores, bookstores and churches, added together. With around 16 whorehouses, including a homosexual one, Consuelo prostitution and nightlife offered many choices.

Trujillo organized many things in the country, and prostitution was one of them. He created the so-called "tolerance zones," or red light districts, to practice the oldest known human profession. Consuelo was so strategically designed that between people's houses and the company's payment office, there were many whorehouses, one beside the other.

Aggressive, toothless, and bony prostitutes stood at the doors of the bars. They would take the workers by their hands, pull them into the place and invite them to have drinks, some fun and forget about life's worries.

Overcoming that temptation did not mean that they would get home with any money. The grocery store owner was also waiting to get his part, because during the week he would sell on credit, waiting to collect on payday.

Most of the men in Consuelo were divided in two basic groups: Those who would get home penniless and drunk because they spent their money with the hookers and those who would get home with mixed feelings of pain and anger, but equally penniless, because the money lenders had kept their cash. Either way, they got home without a dime.

That was life during the period of harvest and production, called zafra, when things were "good." That was the best period of the year for the people of Consuelo.

There were worse ones.

Tiempo Muerto

Tiempo Muerto *(dead time)* was a whole different story.

If no steam came from the boilers, the chimney stopped pouring its constant black smog into the environment, and the whistle didn't sound anymore. That meant Tiempo Muerto had begun. This is the time when the cane grows and the company makes some indispensable repairs for the next zafra. During those months, half the spring, the whole summer, and half of fall, the workers have no source of income, and they live by God's mercy.

In Consuelo, that changed slightly after the 1965 *Revolución de Abril*. An engineer was working on the construction of a new building that was going to change the life of the community. In the process, it also created some badly-needed jobs. To get a job on the construction crew was a matter of fate, not experience. Those interested in working needed to get a number to be included on the waiting list.

The number cost one peso.

Every morning a foreman would spin a rudimentary roulette wheel and those with good fortune would work for a week. On payday, if lucky enough, they might get a couple of bucks and a bottle of booze. During Tiempo Muerto some people survived by harvesting the produce from their yard gardens, if they had planted anything, and on any domesticated animals, such as chickens, goats or pigs. They also fished or caught crabs in the Higuamo river that runs through Consuelo. Hunting helped many people survive while the cane grew and the moneylender waited to collect debts.

Tiempo Muerto always meant more baseball.

During this time of the year, children and grownups indulged in their real passion in life: baseball. Consuelo had two baseball diamonds, one in Pueblo Nuevo and the other close to the corral where the bulls that pulled the cane cart were kept. From early morning, both diamonds were filled with young men, some seeking entertainment and finding stardom, while others were chasing stardom, but didn't get it.

Those were the places where players like Ricardo Carty, *Pepe* Frías, *El Gallo* Batista, Alfredo Griffin, Nelson Norman and many others started out. Thanks to baseball, they escaped the factory life with its circle of poverty, prostitution and money lenders.

In Consuelo, during Tiempo Muerto, baseball practice is like a ritual dance to stimulate the cane to grow. At sunset, they would stop playing because they had no lights on the diamonds, but they did not abandon baseball. The nights of Tiempo Muerto, as well as the finals nights of the zafra, were controlled by the Major League radio sportscasters. Anyone with good ears walking through the streets could "see" every action in the game without needing to stop in any one place. In front of any given house, they used to "see" when Marichal lifted his left foot up to the heavens, from where he would come down with a fireball.

So much emotion was transmitted by the sportscasters that people continued to "see" the game while walking down the streets. They would "see" the player at the batting box fanning at Marichal's pitches, ending up almost kneeling in front of the home plate as if asking for mercy from the merciless Monstruo de Laguna Verde.

Juan Marichal

Archivos Dominicanos

Bottom of the Fourth

The Ga-Gá

El Gallo Batista was never a good runner, but the moment came when he had to be one to score a run. It was not only a run, but also the most important one in his life, even though he did not yet know it. In his legs, under his heavy body, was the run that would break the tie to win, not just the game, but the Dominican national baseball championship. The pitcher on the opposing team, the Leones del Escogido, threw a wild pitch with the bases loaded and the fans of the Estrellas Orientales divided in two groups. From the Grandstand they were pulling him.

"Come on Gallo, come on, you can do it!" they shouted

From the bleachers, they pushed him, "Go Gallo, go. When Gallo's heavy feet landed on home plate, the whole stadium burst into a euphoric explosion. The seventh inning, the lucky seventh for the Estrellas, decided the game and the championship, that February 14, Valentine's Day, in 1968.

Batista scored the run by which the Estrellas won the Dominican championship so long ago that no one remembers it anymore. Three of the most important players on the winning team were from Consuelo: Jaime Davis, Ricardo Carty and Batista. In that playoff, Carty became the first Dominican to hit a home run during a final series. Before, only American players had.

The people of Consuelo were very proud of their boys. During the celebration of the victory and Valentine's Day in 1968, people indulged in a huge bash. Fans of the Estrellas, and those in love, took advantage of the situation and surrendered themselves to a big celebration that many people would remember for months and years to come.

Consuelo was just recovering from the hangover of that big party, Holy Week arrived and, as every year, the Haitians took over the streets of the batey. In the sugarcane plantations, the Easter weekend is like the official Haitian Parade, the time when they exhibit their cultural and religious African roots.

It is Ga-Gá time.

Beginning at midnight, when Thursday ends and Good Friday starts, ritual nerve stimulating drums takes control of the minds, spirits, souls and bodies of many. Their contagious rhythm awakes the batey before sunrise and takes over the streets.

The procession is led by a dancer with a whip in his right hand. He uses it to clear a space, scaring away hostile spirits in the mystical world in which the ritual dance takes place. Before taking the streets, the Ga-Gá priests go to the graveyard to ask the spirits of their ancestors to join the procession. Dancers wear shirts and hats covered with small mirrors, acting as protection against evil spirits. The rationale is that when bad spirits see their horrific shapes in the mirrors, they are terrified by their own ugliness and run away. The dancers carry many multi-colored scarves hanging from their waists, tied with ritual knots. They are red, blue, purple, yellow, green, black and white; they take on new colors resulting from the mix of their sweat and the dust that rises under them as they dance.

The dancers are subjects of a Queen who always wears a spotless white dress, even in the muddiest of paths. Her Majesty and her subjects keep their waists in continuous movement to the rhythm of the drum.

During Ga-Gá times, Consuelo is taken by the rhythm of the drum, a bamboo used as a bass flute, and percussion instruments like maracas and metallic triangles. Under the spell of the music, it is said, many people are spiritually kidnapped. Their bodies are possessed, taken from their homes and dragged for three days of dancing and drinking sugar cane rum under the roasting Caribbean sun. They only let their "hostages" stop to drink some water or have something to eat. Many people, as the stories go, gain back control of their own lives, finding themselves lost in the middle of nowhere. The spiritual kidnappings blamed on the Ga-Gá are famous.

According to the tales, decent women, devoted to their husbands and families are kidnapped. They abandon their homes and spend the weekend dancing Ga-Gá, which is total movement. The people dance while they walk and walk while they dance. The women move their behinds to the rhythm of the drums. Behind them, men dance rubbing their genital area against the female buttocks.

It is a sensual rhythm in which the dancers do not see each other's faces or touch hands. They just feel one another. The only parts of the dancers that touch are the female behind with the male pubic area. Women move ahead in the procession while pushing back their behinds. Men advance, pushing ahead. It is a dance in which waists, butts and thighs are rubbed against each other. In the procession, everyone is half drunk and totally possessed by the madness in the rhythm of the drum, moving forward and backward, bending at their waists, paying no attention to their steps.

The dance has its rules.

Men are not supposed to touch females with their hands without their permission, because it will be interpreted as a terrible act of disrespect. It would be considered almost an attempt to rape her. They dance with their hands up in the air.

Many decent women, possessed by spirits who only care about partying and having fun, spend the weekend in this dance. When they are released from their kidnappers, they go back home to find out they have no husband or family. Those dances have wrecked some homes, at least, for a short period of time.

The Ga-Gá procession starts after midnight on Holy Thursday and ends on Easter Sunday. It takes place during a very difficult spiritual period. It is a dance that has been celebrated by Africans and their descendants since the beginning of slavery. The reason why they do it at that time is simple: Christ is dead, the resurrection has not yet taken place and the slaves refused to worship any dead persons except their ancestors. When Christ is dead, it is the only moment in which the slaves could worship their own Gods and ancestors without conflicting with the ruling Roman Catholic religion.

Missing Someone

The 1968 Major League season was delayed, and in Consuelo, the fans knew that there was a problem because of the assassination of a man called Martin Luther King Jr. It did not mean much to many people in the batey, but the Cocolos were aware of the racial conflicts taking place in the United States. In Consuelo, there was a branch of the "Black Power" movement founded by Jamaican born Marcus Garvey, the leader who organized American blacks in the 1920's Besides that, there were Cocolos from Consuelo living in New York.

Those who did not understand much of what was going on were Dominicans. They knew that only something important would make Americans delay the start of the Major League season.

They were right.

The United States was experiencing serious racial, social and political tensions. That year, when Robert "Bobby" Kennedy was killed, political and racial tension exploded in the streets of Chicago during the Democratic National Convention, as well as in other places of the country and the world. While thousands took to the streets to protest, in the fields of Vietnam 55,000 Americans were being killed.

Without any doubt, 1968 was a year of worldwide political turmoil. "Let's be reasonable; we should demand the impossible," was the major political slogan of the moment.

In the spring of 1968, the Soviet Union took over Czechoslovakia. Student protests broke out in Paris and Mexico City; they were brutally repressed by the police. To this day, Mexicans have many more questions than answers regarding the Tlatelolco massacre in the fall of 1968. In October of that year, Ernesto —Che— Guevara was killed in the mountains of Bolivia, from where his figure rose as a worldwide symbol of rebellion.

In the Major Leagues, 1968 was the year of the pitchers.

When the mound controls the game, the bats are silent. No one, or hardly anyone, gets on base, and no run is scored. The great competition of that year had a Dominican involved. Again, it was, Juan Marichal. His American opponent was Bob Gibson; Sandy Koufax had retired due to problems with his arm.

That year Consuelo's fans felt an emptiness as they listened to the games on the radio; they enjoyed all the action, but something was missing. In 1968 the Club de los Monos (the Monkeys' Club), a group of black Dominicans who had become celebrities in the arts and sports, had two important members missing. Johnny Ventura, the country's leading merengue singer, was sick with hepatitis. The other was Ricardo Carty, who had been diagnosed with tuberculosis during a medical examination prior to spring training. Consuelo's fans grew angry while listening to the games if the sportscaster did not provide constant updates about Carty's health.

Between July and November, in Consuelo, the children who do not play baseball fly kites, or Chichiguas, as they call the flying toys they make using part of dried cane flowers. The Pueblo Nuevo sports field, where the major baseball diamond is, became one of the favorite places for the kids to fly kites. When the sky was crowded with multi-colored kites, the baseball players knew they could cut down a piece of cane to eat and that it was almost time to start the harvest and production season.

Since the end of October, rumors began circulating about an early start of the zafra. The workers who made the repairs always have conflicting versions as to the exact time when the sugar production would start, but it was generally agreed that it would be very soon. New jeeps and other vehicles arrived, and personnel from the harvest department visited the laboratories frequently, taking samples of the cane to test its purity.

The experts advise starting the harvest in November, since it is the month when the sugar cane accumulates more sucrose. November is the month when the cane reaches its highest level of purity. It is the time when the sugar production starts, together with the Dominican baseball season.

Juan Bautista Montero, known by the nickname of Inesito, was one of the few people who knew for sure when the harvest would begin. He arrived in Consuelo from San Juan de la Maguana, about 140 miles southwest of the batey. He plowed the land with a tractor to plant the sugar cane and, when it was ready for harvest, used it to open roads to transport the product.

The afternoon of November12th, 1968, was like any other. Things happened just as usual:

"Amalgama de colores en la pelota
tribuna abierta a toda manifestación deportiva,
dígame que le oigo"
"Amalgam of colors in baseball
open tribune to all sports manifestation
talk to me, that I am listening"

Said Max Reynoso, host of the country's leading afternoon baseball radio talk show.

That day, Inesito's wife, Mireya Sosa, was in labor, exactly nine months after the huge Valentine's Day bash and the victory of the Estrellas Orientales. She was a few steps across the street from the home plate where Ricardo Carty, Rafael Batista, Pepe Frías, Alfredo Griffin and Julio Franco, practiced batting every day. There she delivered her son. The couple was so poor that they did not even have a name, so they gave him a nickname: Maiky.

The world would later know him as Sammy Sosa.

A few weeks later, it was the Cocolos' turn to take over the streets, jamming and dancing in a mix of religious and folkloric procession. The dancers carried long peacock feathers adorning their hats and small mirrors on their shirts, just as the Haitians. Cocolos performed many dances.

The Guloyas, as called by Dominicans, is the most popular. It represented the ancestral tale of the small and weak overcoming the big and strong. One big dancer has all sorts of wood-carved weapons and a smaller one runs around with just a stick and a piece of rope. They portray the combat between David and Goliath, keeping alive the faith that someday, somewhere, somehow, the little guy will finally be able to overcome any difficulty, no matter how big, including defeating very big guys. During the day, the Guloyas took to the streets and after dark they belonged to the musicians.

"Good Morning, Good Morning give me my guavaberry"

sang the jamming Cocolos that started playing music and drinking at sunset. They kept on until sunrise, going from house to house requesting a drink of Guavaberry, a delicious mix of wild Caribbean berries with sugarcane rum.

The Guloyas and their moving parties always took over the streets of Consuelo in the fall of the year, announcing that Christmas was just around the corner.

5th Inning

Top of the Fifth

Struggling for Life

In 1969, men walked on the moon for the first time.

And an important Dominican radio network was created to broadcast baseball games. Billy Berroa, Freddy Mondesí, Johnny Naranjo and Lilín Díaz, founded La Gran Cadena de la Calidad, covering the entire island. Their voices transmitted the emotions of every action in the games, inspiring an uncountable number of young men to play baseball.

Maiky was only a year old when the roulette stopped, the bets ended and no one ever again collected booze as wages for their work. The construction ended. Consuelo's first public school was built, funded by the Alliance for Progress, created by President John F. Kennedy. The school, Escuela Divina Providencia (Divine Providence), which has been administered since its foundation by Canadian Roman Catholic nuns, offered elementary and junior high school education to thousands of children. Until then, they did not have any option for quality education.

Divina Providencia School, run by sisters Ann Nolan and Leonor Gibb, is the best public school in the Dominican Republic and perhaps in Latin America. It is the institution with which Consuelo started the process of modernization.

The moneylenders did not lag behind.

They caught up with modernization, developing a new line of business intimately connected to the poverty of their victims. They bought grocery stores and evolved from the old practice of lending physical money; they introduced what could be called a rudimentary version of the credit card. The workers who wanted to borrow money got a credit line through purchase orders, which they called vale (a Spanish expression for worth). Vale was the name the people gave to the financial instrument they created, because all the notes started out with the word vale as a way of expressing their intrinsic worth.

The moneylenders' grocery stores had the highest prices, but only there could the workers redeem the infamous vales. Paying for the groceries in that way was only a part of the workers' obligations and responsibilities. They also had to pay interest on the borrowed money they never saw, and for the food they ate the previous week. In such places, people paid interest for the food they had already digested and expelled from their bodies, but thanks to ignorance, they didn't figure that out.

Padre José was long gone, but his legacy prevailed.

The co-op responded to the moneylenders by enlarging their food warehouse and marking down their prices. It also loaned money to the workers at a very low interest rate and sold groceries on credit, without interest, and at affordable prices. The increase in those services created a demand for new ones and opened the window for other people to make some money.

He was not really dressed.

He just pretended to be, using what was once a pair of pants barely covering his childish genitalia and buttocks, barefooted and shirtless. He pulled and pushed a cart up and down the rocky and dusty streets of Consuelo, providing delivery services for the workers and their families that shopped at the co-op. That was how Julio Franco, then eleven years old, earned a couple of pesos every Saturday morning. At noon he returned home, to give his mother the money, have a bite of whatever was there for a meal and was back on the streets. Saturday was payday, and he took advantage of it. In the afternoon he made a lot more money and even got some fresh meat for dinner.

He would go to the gallera, the cockfighting arena.

The best fights with the highest bets were held in the afternoon. In the gallera almost every man carried long machetes hanging from their waists or long, sharp knives "hidden," but visible under their shirts. In their pockets they carried a bottle of rum and in their mouths a cachimbo (pipe) or a pachuché, a strong and oily cigar of natural tobacco that they rolled up according to the taste of each smoker. The afternoons were filled with the sound of a Perico Ripiao, a band of musicians playing typical merengue, to the rhythm of drums, güira, maracas and accordions.

Every spectator at the gallera gathered around the rudimentary wooden coliseum, shaped as an arena, to see one cockfight after the other. It is a wonder cock fighting had not been declared the Dominican National Sport. Every Saturday the cock fights awakened new emotions even though the cocks kept fighting for the same unknown reason that made them fight since the beginning of time.

Outside the arena, the Perico Ripiao sounds had everyone dancing, and the machetes could be seen moving at their own rhythm, hanging from the waists of the dancers. The stains of sweat were visible under the armpits of the men's khaki shirts. Most of the women who frequented the gallera dressed in flowered designs and vivid shades of blue, green, yellow, and red. They danced to the music of the band. Every Saturday the gallera was the most important social gathering for many villagers. While some listened to the music, drank and danced, others enjoyed the fights while listening to the baseball game in battery-powered transistor radios. The cockfights usually finished with a dead animal. The depressed owner, after losing his money, hopes and cock, needed to go through another difficult procedure. He had to go to the barbwire fence and hand over the blood-dripping, dead animal to a few boys equipped with razor blades and fine thread.

They took the dead cock, hung it by its feet on the fence, and after a few cuts at strategic points of the body, quickly skinned the entire animal.

Julio Franco was one of those boys.

Many Saturdays, besides money, he came home with a baja, the animals killed in combat. It always made for a good meal. He spent the weekdays going up and down Consuelo streets peddling finger food that his mother prepared.

This was before Maiky was even able to walk.

The Giant Laurel Trees

Maiky spent the first years of his life in Pueblo Nuevo, under the thick shadow of the Ficus, a giant laurel tree brought to Consuelo from New England during the time of Mr. Kilbourne. More than herbs for cooking, these laurel trees offered plenty of shade from the burning Caribbean sun. The yard of the Parroquia Santa Ana and almost all the streets of Pueblo Nuevo have giant laurel trees planted around them. Across from the house where Maiky was born is the Club Los Laureles.

The thick shield from the sun that the giant laurels offer is not free for women, like Maiky's mom, who needed to keep their yards clean. Every tree produces an uncountable number of little balls of a pale, lifeless shade of gray. A caterpillar-like bright red worm, called gongorochos, feeds on the Ficus ball once it hits the ground. The streets of Pueblo Nuevo at times are filled with those little balls and gongorochos chasing them.

Under those trees, the nights are darker, thicker and longer, so long that some seem endless. One night, Inesito fell ill and was rushed into a car that smashed gongorochos and little Ficus balls all the way out of Consuelo. He was taken to a hospital in Santo Domingo, almost two hours away. Silence deserted Pueblo Nuevo, the dogs howled like wolves in the distance, or burst into ferocious fights with God only knows what animal. The cats fought or made love. In any case, they made a lot of noise and sounded as if they were talking and screaming at each other. The little balls of the giant laurels fell constantly on the metal roof of the house.

It was a long, wide and thick night.

That night, without an obituary in the newspaper or announcement on the radio, without wake or rosary, and even without a burial ceremony, Inesito faded away. He never came back. He was buried in "Los Jovillos," a rural section in the Azua province, almost 150 miles west of Consuelo.

His son, Maiky, was then seven years old.

In 1975 a lot of important things happened to baseball in

the Dominican Republic and in the U.S.

In Santo Domingo, pitcher Pedro Borbón won two games in which the opposing team, the Aguilas Cibaeñas, did not score any runs. Thanks to his performance his team, the Tigres del Licey, won the National Championship.

Cesarín Gerónimo, known as the Jefe Indio (Indian Chief) in Dominican baseball, won a Golden Glove and hit two home runs helping the Cincinnati Reds to win the World Series that year. Everyone agreed that Gerónimo had one of the strongest and most gifted arms in baseball.

On April the 17th, 1975, Juan Marichal took voluntary retirement, after a fruitful career. His perennial childish smile disappeared from the mound the same year in which baseball began to lose its innocence.

At the end of that year, an old feud between players and team owners was finally settled. A court ruling recognized the players' status as "Free Agents." The old-style contract system ended, and the players became millionaires. Too much gold proved to be bad for people unprepared to handle it.

A big abyss began to separate players and fans; it grew bigger and bigger, as new millionaire players signed the fat contracts every year. Many players quit being heroes and became greedy, arrogant and nasty human beings.

In 1975, one of the game's best-paid players entered the world. On July 27, Alex Rodríguez was born.

Bottom of the Fifth

First Training

Soaking in sweat and half-dehydrated after running from one base to another, Consuelo's children hide from the burning sun under the giant laurels. They chew sugarcane, recover a little fluid in their system and get a natural dose of sugar. The sweet juice slides down their throats as the best antidote against the heat and exhaustion.

Fatherless at seven, Maiky was poorly fed, barefooted and shirtless, exposing his ash-like black skin stained by the sun. The remnants of a pair of pants that once belonged to someone unknown to him hung from his waist.

He wanted candies like any other child, but no one would buy them for him. He wanted toys, but that was only a wishful dream; he was hungry, trying to calm his demanding stomach.

His first training was part of his survival technique. There are very lucky kids whose parents go to the candy store and buy them all sorts of goodies. There are others who have no one to buy them anything, but they do not have it worse in life just because of that. The sugar in the candies drives children wild, and Maiky wasn't an exception. While rich kids take chemically-treated sugar, loaded with artificial components, Maiky enjoyed natural sugar, direct from the source, chewing the sugarcane.

He spent whole days chasing trucks loaded with sugar cane, wrapped in a cloud of dust that rose as the trucks passed. The street where he was born is probably among the dustiest in the entire country, and the kids who live there suffer repeatedly from respiratory infections.

Maiky had a constant stream of mucus running from his nose. To make things worse, there was barely any sunshine on his street. On each side there was a row of giant laurels. Their branches joined over the middle of the street, creating a ceiling-like cover that kept the sunshine out and a fair amount of dust continually floating. Chasing the trucks in that dusty bubble, Maiky may have started developing the necessary speed to steal bases in the Majors. It may have felt like a game to him from the very beginning. To be able to run as fast as the truck, and even beat it, was the first challenge; to pull out a cane while the truck was moving was the next. His reward was the sweet juice of the cane, his natural candy.

After eating candy, kids play, driven by the sugar stimulation, and Maiky wanted to play, but at first glance it seemed he had no toys. When he finished chewing the piece of cane, he would spit the tasteless spongy remains, called bagazo, up in the air and try to bat it with the piece of cane kept in his hand. Thus he started his batting practice. The sugar cane was his candy, his energy source, his toy and his only companion for a long while.

Also, to avoid starving, he threw rocks into a mango tree. This was the beginning practice for his strong arm. When he was not chasing trucks, he was flinging stones up into the mango tree in the yard of Club los Laureles.

Sometimes he would go to The Play, as the baseball diamond across the street from his house is called. There he connected with baseball. By then his older brother, Luis, spent a lot of time there. He was one of many youngsters in Consuelo who dreamed of following in the footsteps of Carty, Batista, Pepe Frías, and others. Maiky's next door neighbor, Ramón —Mon— Carty was playing for Estrellas Orientales. On his same dusty street, in the mid-70s, at least two boys were signed to play professional ball; Luis thought that his contract was just around the corner. At this time, Maiky was chasing trucks, chewing sugar cane, spitting up the bagazo and hitting it with the cane.

The Widow

After her husband passed away, Mireya also lost the trust she had in certain members of her own family. She discovered which friends were real friends and which ones were just pretending. She found many men wanting to take advantage of her needs and trying to get her sexual favors. She was now mother *and* father to her children: Luis, Negrón, Magaly, Raquel, Niño and Maiky, as well as five children that her late husband brought from his home town of San Juan de la Maguana. She had to feed them or, at least, give them something to fool their stomachs, to calm their hunger. To feed eleven children without a job or the means of getting one is, indeed, quite a challenge.

Mireya felt as if she were under siege by the hyenas of disgrace. She was a young widow. Many potential mates with more or less good intentions were offering to help her with her huge family responsibility. She had to make a decision, choose which path to follow, which proposal to accept. One night she took a pencil and paper, and prepared a list. She put the names of those who were propositioning her beside numbers that at first sight seemed to have no logical order.

Those would be her customers.

The following morning, the 5:30 whistle woke up the rooster, and the rooster woke up Mireya. She awoke only with "the grace of God and water from the faucet." She placed the folded list of her suitors and future customers between her breast and her bra, and set out into the street, her mind was made up.

She would sell what everyone wanted.

The Sales

In 1974, the Dominican opposition parties united in one block against President Balaguer: but they denounced electoral fraud before the elections were held and withdrew from the voting. That year, as in many other years, the country's democracy survived its politicians. The government knew it had no popular support and saw in each citizen a possible enemy; and with good reason. To protect himself from the growing number of "enemies," Balaguer shared power with the highly politicized and right wing controlled military and police institutions. He granted them absolute control of the streets.

In that environment, armed with her list and a pen, Mireya set out for the street.

She started to peddle hope.

She charged each customer 35 cents in exchange for the chance to win $20 Dominican pesos if they had the lucky number in the national lottery. Many women, mostly single mothers, made a living that way. The people call them riferas. The $20 pesos that she offered as a prize was more than the weekly take home pay of those earning the minimum wage of $3.20 per day.

The informal hope peddlers were arrested by the police, as they are today, because it is an illegal way of privatizing and profiting from the National Lottery. That was why they hid their lists in their bras. The police often presented the list in court as evidence of their offense. In the past, officers put their hands all over the riferas' breasts looking for the evidence. The women protested this invasion of privacy and violation of their bodies, assuming it was an attempt to rape them. They usually had community support for their protest.

The riferas were highly appreciated by a community of grateful patrons who had won money with them, and by those keeping alive the hope of hitting their small jackpot. Those women were the only ones to deliver good news to the majority of the population. That is why people protected them from the police in any way, including providing them with a hideout to avoid being arrested. Besides troubles with the police, to peddle hope is a risky and complicated business filled with hypocrisy. As Mireya's customers bet on a kind of "pick two" drawing, she made up a list of 100 numbers. She really did not want anyone to win the prize, because when that happened she ended up with very little money. She, like any other rifera, would rather sell all the numbers except the lucky one, so then she could keep all the money. If that happened too often, her reputation would be terribly affected, since the word would get around that no one ever won with her. People would then stop buying hope from her. No one is more superstitious than a gambler.

Mireya needed to keep her customers' faith alive that they would hit the jackpot but, by the same token, she prayed in silence for that not to happen.

In those days, hope began to vanish from the Dominican

Republic. The National Lottery had only one weekly drawing on Sunday and the non-winners, the vast majority of the people, would wait until the next week to try their luck again. That is why some visionary of the rifa business decided to import hope. They started to peddle numbers for people to try their luck in the daily lotteries from Venezuela. Those drawings could clearly be heard on Dominican radio.

That business is called caraquita, which is a diminutive of Caracas, the Venezuelan capital. Mireya walked up and down Consuelo's streets offering hope. She peddled both those from caraquita and the National Lottery. Besides, she also had a bingo game going on at her home as a way to make a little more money.

The Runaway

A year after the death of Inesito, Mireya was free of her stepchildren, since they took off to live their own lives. Then she decided to accept one of her admirers. It was Carlos Peralta, a driver of one of the trucks Maiky chased every day to get sugarcane.

Carlos did not come alone. He brought two children.

The increase in the family size also increased the demand for food. The raffle and bingo were not very profitable and were also sources of trouble with the police.

One day, Mireya and Carlos fled Consuelo.

Poor people don't move from one house to another; they just run away from poverty, which is why they do it at night. Perhaps they think that poverty is sleeping and they can escape it. In the darkness of the night, they avoid their neighbors, equally poor but gossips, being able to see their torn and worn-out belongings that expose their poverty. Honoring this tradition, as old as hunger itself, Mireya and Carlos packed their children, un-belongins, and fled Consuelo.

Maiky suspended his training.

He wouldn't run around chasing the trucks anymore; he was taken away from the baseball diamond across from which he was born.

The family started a sort of nomadic life, a pilgrimage, looking for their own promised land.

6th Inning

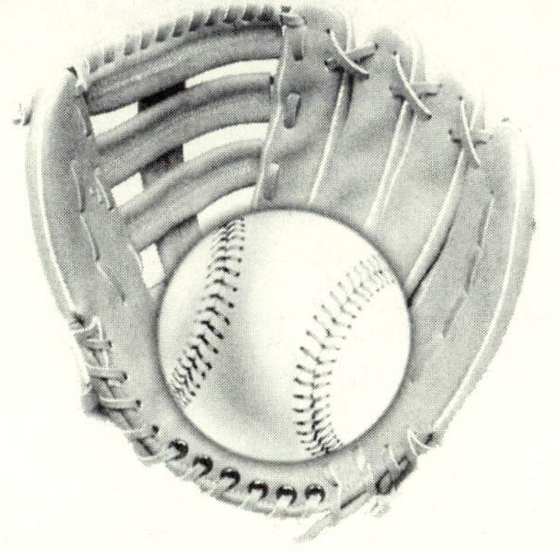

Top of the Sixth

The Road is the Destiny

Sitting in the truck's cab, Mireya felt relief as she left Consuelo behind to begin a new life, far away from the memories of her late husband. After driving among the many cane fields for a while, she and her family ended up in the countryside of a rural town called Bayaguana. They stayed there a short time, then moved to another sugarcane plantation called Ingenio San Luis, 15 miles east of Santo Domingo. Mireya did not have to sweep the little balls from the giant laurel trees anymore, nor the gongorochos that chased them. She wouldn't have to pour pans of water on her yard or on the street in front of her home to reduce the dust in the air.

In San Luis, there wasn't any street that was as dusty as "B" street in Consuelo. Rather, the entire San Luis area was like a huge dustpan. The place had more dust and whorehouses than Consuelo, and it did not even have a decent baseball diamond.

It was never clear if poverty followed them from Consuelo, or if it was omnipresent and met them there. Perhaps they packed it with their un-belongings.

Mireya was with Carlos, her children and her poverty.

Carlos was the kind of man who belonged on the road, a truck driver with thousands and thousands of miles behind him and thousands more to go. They decided to continue their flight and took off for their new home: the road. They packed whatever they could and went into the capital city, Santo Domingo. Here Maiky would begin his career in the informal work force and become a number in statistics about child labor. With a rudimentary wooden box and some supplies for shoe polishing, he spent long hours in the Parque Enriquillo, the main park of Villa Francisca, a Santo Domingo slum.

To be poor in the capital city is a lot worse than to be poor on the plantation. In Villa Francisca, finally, they were living on paved streets; they escaped the dust but had not arrived in paradise.

In their new home, they had no water.

They walked many blocks up and down the hills of the barrio looking for a broken pipe on the sidewalk in order to get some water. They lived in a backyard without the little balls from the giant laurel trees and without dust, but in their new home, poverty was bolder and fleshless. In Villa Francisca, houses had toilets, but most of them had no running water. People lived in old wooden houses rotted out by termites. They used pieces of cardboard rescued from trashcans to cover as many holes as they could, to ensure some privacy.

In Villa Francisca, they lived close to the station where buses departed to San Pedro de Macorís. All day long, the assistant driver, hanging on the door trying to get passengers, cried out his destination.

"San Pedro, San Pedro, Macorís, Macorís."

For Mireya, it was an invitation to go back to San Pedro. There, at least she had some relatives and would be closer to her girlfriends in Consuelo. By then, Villa Francisca, like all the other shantytowns in the outskirts of Santo Do-mingo, was a battlefield for an increasingly bloody and undeclared war. Government popularity plunged by the day, and the opposition was armed. They took to the streets and, in response, the government increased police repression.

In those days, it was common to wake up in the morning and learn your neighbor was found in a drainage pit with "his mouth filled with flies" after being executed the previous evening by the police or paramilitary death squads. The opposition would then kill a couple of police officers, and the police in turn would shoot whoever remotely seemed to be an enemy.

Youth were considered enemies of the government by virtue of being young; their lives were in danger without having done anything to anyone. Luis, the eldest of the Sosa family, was walking a tight rope because of his age.

The very death they had been trying to get away from was closer now than ever before.

If the family stayed there, they could have died from starvation or any of the countless illnesses that sprouted around the unhealthy backyards of the barrio. If they survived those dangers, they could very well have been hit by stray bullets that had become "frequent flyers" in the darkness of Villa Francisca's nights. During that time, the police and the armed opposition engaged in gunfights on any corner, at any given time. The danger increased, and the bus driver's assistant kept on calling:

"San Pedro, San Pedro, Macorís, Macorís."

It was time to go. Again.

Mireya and Carlos returned to the road. They packed and set out for San Pedro de Macorís. The family was completing a circle; they were returning to their point of departure. This time, without knowing it, they were keeping an appointment with their destiny.

That Guy

They ended up in Barrio Lindo, a place that did not honor its name. Lindo means "pretty", but this barrio was the opposite, since it was situated in the middle of one of San Pedro's slums. They lived close to a huge and infamous whorehouse: El 80. All day long loud music emanated from the site, disturbing the neighbors' peace, "only" 24-hours a day. At night, the hookers and their customers controlled the entire area.

The place became so famous that its name was adopted as a stop for the town bus service. It was a place well known to the ER personnel of the local hospital due to the frequency with which some customers ended up stabbed in fights. Those fights were scandalous. Maiky would pass in front of the place at least twice a day in the morning when he set out and then in the afternoon when he returned after making a few bucks doing different chores.

His sisters were in puberty in an environment under the total control of El 80. Everyone suffered the scandals and was exposed to the danger, but the owners had connections with local authorities. There was no way of closing it down, at least so it was thought, until the religious community decided to take action, launching an attack with a rumor, and closing it down with gossip.

One night, as the story goes, a strange customer showed up at El 80. He asked for a couple of bottles of rum, and drank the entire contents in a few minutes. He sat at a table and called a few hookers with whom he drank. Then he walked out and went to a stand where an old lady was selling fried chicken, plantains, and other food. He ate all that was there for sale. The stranger had a mysterious and wide smile, making it easy to see his many golden teeth.

Then he stood up to dance.

He was such an impressive dancer, that everyone stopped to watch him. No doubt about it, he was a star. His performance revealed who this strange customer was. He kept up with the rhythm of the music, and those who tried to imitate the new steps discovered his real identity. His feet never touched the floor and, once people took the time to look at them, they looked at each other in disbelief.

This fellow had goat feet.

Yes, a man with goat feet!

It was the devil himself, with the long tail and fire in his eyes, who showed up that night at El 80 and, according to the story, promised to come back. Every night.

The church circulated that story and it spread as fast as any gossip, as quick as lighted gunpowder. El 80 ended up bankrupt.

It was OK that they were sinners, we all are, but they had no interest in getting together with the devil himself.

Mireya and her family lived around the corner from the whorehouse, and their lives were as bad as they had always been, or perhaps, even a little worse. Pushed by the same old poverty, and now scared by the presence of the devil in their lives, the family returned to the road.

Closer to the Beginning

While they were in Santo Domingo, the government closed a public health station in San Pedro de Macorís. It was a one-story rectangular building filled with little working spaces where bioanalysts spent the day hanging over their microscopes analyzing all kinds of samples. It also had a couple of rooms with stretchers to conduct medical examinations and a few administrative offices.

When Carlos, Mireya and their children returned to San Pedro de Macorís, the former health station had become a new home for the homeless, a group to which they belonged. They were fortunate to find a friend from Consuelo who helped them get a couple of empty spaces, which became their new home.

Only five miles separated them now from Consuelo.

The street in front of the old building was totally destroyed by the construction of a new drainage system that took many years to finish. Trucks loaded with sugarcane on their way to any of the six sugar factories surrounding San Pedro were always passing in front of their new home. Others passed loaded with sugar to be shipped from the local harbor to the U.S. and other international markets. As all families that have chosen the road as their home, the Peralta-Sosa family settled in that place, but were ready to leave at anytime.

They had a view of a bus station and a taxi stand.

In front of their new home there were always cars and buses that traveled to Consuelo, Hato Mayor, El Seibo, and other towns in the Eastern part of the island. The side street is a beltline avenue through which tourists pass on their way to La Romana and other tourist destinations in the region. The old building, although not comfortable, served a great purpose in their lives. It was the only roof they could find far from the devil's dwelling place. This new home brought Maiky very close to his destiny. Those unstable years were preparing him for the future, though he did not yet know it.

Bottom of the Sixth

Between Two Diamonds

Poverty is filled with mysterious forces.

At times, it seemed to take Maiky away from his destiny. He did not carry his "bread under his arm," as other children. No one argues that. But at least he had it across the street from where he was born, in a baseball diamond filled with history. His family took him away from that field when they started their life's pilgrimage. They now had ended up between two diamonds.

The Estadio Tetelo Vargas, home of the Estrellas Orientales, the local baseball team, is across the street from the old building were they moved. A few blocks behind is the Play de Barrio México, known in professional baseball as a place from which very good players are harvested.

The walls of the old building, an almost four feet high cement fence, were decorated by the children. They demonstrated that even in the most abject poverty, it is possible to have fun, and they left behind vivid reminders of their existence. There were an enormous number of mud stains on the walls. Anyone would have thought that the building had been attacked with mud bombs, but that was not the case. The stains surrounded a black circle, hand-drawn with charcoal.

In the abandoned public health station, now Maiky's family home, they lived close to the main entrance of the building. Whenever Maiky went in and out, there were children playing a baseball game that stained the walls. One would stand with a stick or whatever they could use as a bat, another served as pitcher with a ball made out of old socks and the charcoal circle painted on the wall served as a motionless catcher and the strike zone.

If the batter let the ball pass and it fell in the circle, it was a strike, and three strikes equal a strikeout. The pitcher would then become the batter and the kid at bat would take the pitcher's post. All day long, there were children playing *el ponchao*, the game they played on the walls of the old building's fence.

On rainy days, the balls made out of old socks would fall in the potholes filled with muddy water and, when they hit the wall, would leave their permanent tracks as a mud stain. Many times those wet balls resolved disputes and conflicting opinions regarding whether a pitch was a ball or a strike. The mark on the wall avoided arguments. When those walls became useless because of too many mud stains, the children looked for other ones, such as those of the Estadio Tetelo Vargas across the street.

El ponchao is not the only way of playing baseball these kids developed. The stadium's front parking lot is a place were children spend the whole day playing *el que apara batea*, meaning, "the one who catches the ball will be the next to bat." One child takes the bat, another is the pitcher and all the rest try to catch the ball, putting out the kid at bat. That is the only way in which they can get a turn to bat. The best hitter could bat many times before being put out.

Sometimes, Maiky stopped to play *el ponchao or el que apara batea*, but he was always in a hurry. He was attracted to the game, but needed to survive and contribute to his family's welfare. He had no time to stop and play as the other kids. Poverty and its urgencies were about to take away the only thing he had left: his childhood.

The Night

Old abandoned buildings don't have electric services but, strangely enough, Maiky and his family had lights on certain nights. The town of San Pedro de Macorís was left in the dark, instead using the energy to illuminate the Tetelo Vargas stadium during game nights. While the rest of the city's population was in the dark, Maiky's family's home was totally illuminated with a powerful light from the stadium across the street.

Baseball has always brought light to their lives.

Summer nights, however, were awful and dark; the ball

season was over. In their home, the heat was literally suffocating for the people packed in their narrow spaces. They were forced to get out, hoping for fresh air, but once outside a swarm of mosquitoes ambushed them. They were forced to retreat to their narrow little roasting rooms to bear the unbearable heat, almost boiling in their own sweat. The mosquitoes chased them in, and once they were against the wall, there was no escape. The bugs, like thirsty little vampires, sucked out their blood as they stung their victims' hot, wet skin. In that place, people do not sleep. They spend their nights in a constant fight that almost always is won by the mosquitoes. If on any given night, the thirsty little vampires gave them a break, that did not mean quiet time.

Pena, es lo que siento en mi alma
porque esa mujer no entiende
y me hace perder la calma

Pain is what I feel in my soul
because this woman doesn't understand
and she makes me lose my calmness

So goes the lyrics of a popular Dominican song of Luis Segura, El Añoñaito (The Spoiled Little Brat). It is a song of a male complaint against his lover who does not understand him and makes him lose his temper. The song was part of a another genre in Dominican popular music, the lyrics telling dramatic stories of unsuccessful love obsessions. The Bachata was capturing Dominicans' hearts and imaginations but, in the process, was taking away the quiet time Maiky's family needed to sleep.

Between the wall of their room and the side avenue, there were huts in which cheap prostitution business took place all night long. Even if they did not want to, they spent the night listening to bachatas. There was a constant fight inside the old building. Residents fought to protect their spaces from incoming homeless. In the whorehouses, there were always fights that many times ended up with slain customers.

People who go to sleep on the floor really do not "lay down." They just throw themselves down in the night, and after dawn, instead of "getting up," they just stand up. In the morning, the residents of the old building stood up with pains all over their bodies because of the many times they had beaten themselves trying to kill the mosquitoes. Exhausted, sleepy and missing a few milliliters of blood, they needed to start their day. They left with blood stains on their skin were they killed a mosquito, and many left with dead mosquitoes hanging from their dried, blood-stained skin.

During daytime, the mosquitoes would go away, but then came the trucks, cars, buses, and other vehicles around the bus stop and taxi stand. Horns and voices of motorists, insulting each other, and drivers' assistants announcing departures and destinations of their vehicles controlled the entire day. It did not matter how sleepy they were. During daytime the residents of the old building needed to get out because the heat and noise inside were simply unbearable. During the seventies and the late eighties, while Maiky and his family lived in that building, many things happened in the world of baseball.

The decade of the 1970's started out very well.

In 1970, Ricardo Carty became Consuelo's first batting champion in the National League after hitting .366.

1977 was very important for Latin America: one of the most important treaties in modern world history was signed in Panamá. General Omar Torrijos, the Panamanian head of state, convinced President Jimmy Carter to return the canal to Panama at the end of 1999. That was one of the most important Latin American political victories of the century.

Panamá celebrated it in the Majors.

Rod Carew was born in Gatún, the Canal Area in Panamá. He was playing with the Minnesota Twins, and at the end of the 1977 Major League season he had 239 hits, 16 doubles, and scored 128 runs, leading the league in each of those categories. The same year the canal treaty was signed, Carew became the first, and as yet the only Panamanian, to become the Most Valuable Player for the American League. He was the second Latin American player honored by that distinction.

Shortly thereafter, a political crisis that had been brewing in Guatemala since 1954 spread to other countries. The entire Central American region burst into political turmoil and military conflicts, forcing hundreds of thousands of Guatemaleans, Hondurans, Salvadoreans and Nicaraguans to seek refuge in the United States.

In 1977, Martín Dihigo, who was born in Matanzas, Cuba, on May 24, 1905, was inducted into the Hall of Fame in Cooperstown, New York. He was a legendary player. During a championship in Mexico in 1938, the same year in which Marichal was born, Dihigo pitched 20 games and won 18. As if this were not enough, in the same season he was the batting champion with a .388 average. He died in Cienfuegos, Cuba, the land for which he always professed an unconditional love, six years before being inducted in the Hall of Fame. In 1977, Dominican Franklin Taveras stole 77 bases. Between 1972 and 1978 the "Super Baby", César Cedeño, the Houston Astros' star, won five Golden Gloves and the Jefe Indio, Cesarín Gerónimo, took four.

Joaquín Balaguer lost the Dominican elections in 1978 and turned over power to the winning candidate, ending 12 years of political difficulties for the country. From then on, it was no longer necessary for the police to defend the government; the people themselves took on that job. Political crime ended, and the country started a new era of political freedom under the government of President Antonio Guzmán.

The following year, 1979, another Cocolo from Consuelo was highly distinguished. Alfredo Griffin was the first Dominican to become Rookie of the Year in the American League, while playing with the Toronto Blue Jays. The same year Nelson Norman, another Cocolo from Consuelo, who lived a couple of blocks from Maiky, led his Dominican team, the Aguilas Cibaeñas, to victory in the national championship. During that playoff, Norman got 12 hits, including two doubles and one triple, in 21 at bats, for a .571 average. Until now, no one has done anything like that in a Dominican final playoff.

As the seventies came to a close, there were 50 Dominicans in the Majors, whose lives were changed forever by baseball. Hundreds of them were in the minors, training and waiting to be called up to the Majors. As soon as possible.

Dominican players would continue to provide great surprises and thrills in Major Leagues and to baseball fans worldwide.

Jorge Bell, the first Dominican to win an MVP award. The former manager of the Estrellas Orientales and First Dominican Rookie of the Year, Alfredo Griffin. Pedro Guerrero La Negra Pola and Cesarín El Jefe Indio Gerónimo.

7th Inning

Top of the Seventh

The Stolen Childhood

"Señor, ¿va a limpiar?"

"Are you getting your shoes shined, sir?"

The sweet voice came from the dark face of a child, his dried lips a symptom of his near dehydration. His eyes sunk deep into his face, as if starvation were eating them from the inside. His black skin was ashen, as if poverty were taking away the only thing he had left: his color.

Between his left arm and body he carried a rustic wooden box with polish, brushes, cloths and other working tools. An empty paint can hung from his right arm, on which he sat to do his job.

The remains of what was once a shirt, much older than he was, hung buttonless from his shoulders. Some cloth strips he called pants were barely covering him. His stained bare feet were easily confused with the dirty ground of Parque Duarte, San Pedro de Macorís' Central Park.

Maiky went there, not to polish shoes, but to survive.

The shoe polishing business in that park was a kind of a monopoly controlled by an experienced and well-connected shoe polisher called Morocotas. He was an entrepreneur and an artist. While he polished his customers' shoes, he used his brush and box, as musical instruments, executing the rhythm of the most popular merengue or salsa. He was the major shoe shiner in the park, with loyal customers, and even had people on a "waiting list" for his services. Sometimes Morocotas had to "sub-contract" work to other shoe polishers and become their supervisor.

Morocotas controlled the northeast corner of the park, the intersection of Avenida Independencia and Calle Rafael Deligne. What was not under his control was in the hands of another shoe polisher who had no name because he did not need one. Even if you were to call him he could not hear you because he was deaf. In the southwest corner of the park, there were always many compulsive gamblers betting on everything. They would even bet on whether the license plate of the next incoming vehicle would end in an even or an odd number. They called that game "la plaquita," which means "the little license plate." The southeastern corner of the park was where grown-up alcoholics and gasoline-sniffing children spent their days. Besides drugs, alcohol and gambling, there were serious problems of child homosexual prostitution in the park.

Maiky survived in the northeast corner of the park.

The possibilities of finding customers to polish shoes became harder due to the expansion of Morocotas' monopoly, and Maiky was forced to diversify his line of services. He washed and watched over cars parked in the northeast corner of the park. He helped many people who survived with fruit, food, candies and cigarette peddling stands. The owners of those stands trusted him and would leave him in charge of their businesses while they took a lunch or a bathroom break. That also meant that he could have free oranges, pineapple, or cantaloupe slices, or even an egg sandwich, as his first meal of the day.

From his corner of the park, Maiky watched when Jorge Bell, Joaquín Andújar and other Major League stars parked their luxurious cars and walked by. By then, perhaps his highest ambition was to one day become a successful shoe polisher like Morocotas or, in a different dream, to be able to wash the car of a Major League star.

There was something he knew by then.

Like many other Dominicans, he wanted to live in the United States. Some Dominican Yorks, referring to those living in New York City, often showed up at the park showing off borrowed clothes or pieces of jewelry, rented only to impress people like Maiky.

The nicest things he had seen came from the United States, and there was no doubt in his mind.

He wanted to go there.

A New Path

While Maiky washed and watched over cars or polished shoes in the Parque Duarte, many important things happened in San Pedro de Macorís and the Majors. Pedro Guerrero, another player from San Pedro, led the Los Angeles Dodgers to win the World Series in 1981. That year the "Negra Pola" as he was called, was chosen the MVP of the World Series, and Jorge Bell was brought up to the Majors. The following year another player from the town, Joaquín Andújar, won two of the games by which the St. Louis Cardinals won the 1982 World Series.

All those players parked their luxurious cars across the Parque Duarte, and Maiky wanted to wash them.

He was dreaming of a good tip.

At the end of every game in San Pedro's Estadio Tetelo Vargas, many fans stopped in the Dugout. This was a restaurant where they gathered to drink beer and talk about the game. From that place, many radio talk shows were broadcast live. The restaurant was across the Parque Duarte in a strange corner formed by three streets: the avenues Independencia and 27 de Febrero. The latter was the only way of getting from San Pedro to La Romana. Both streets are parallel, running east and west. The third in this tri-street corner was General Cabral that runs north and south.

Every time a customer was finished, leaving food on his plate, it was taken to the kitchen. Part of the ethics of poverty is an unwritten rule that forbids throwing away any portion of food that could feed one of so many hungry people. Maiky satisfied part of his food needs thanks to this tradition. The days when he got a good meal in the restaurant's kitchen, he also could save more money to take home.

He left behind the old abandoned building between the two baseball diamonds for the Parque Duarte and entered baseball through the door by which only the very best entered the game: the Dugout. Besides that restaurant, he also ate in the kitchen of one of the most famous and traditional restaurants in San Pedro, the BBYVT, which in Spanish is a combination of words that sounds like "Drink and Go."

The very best day can be ruined in a second for a street

kid like Maiky, and many times what seems to be a lucky strike can turn out to be exactly the opposite. One day he entered the kitchen of the Dugout and thought it was his lucky day. There was almost a whole steak left by a customer. He took it without asking for permission, not because of lack of manners, but because everyone there knew him, and that he ate on those opportunities. He was about to put it into his mouth, when the steak jumped from his hands and, as if he were chasing it, he ran after it.

He was not trying to catch it, he was running away.

Someone struck him in the back with the edge of a big restaurant tray. He ran from the kitchen as the sound of the tray striking his back echoed in his head and became confused with a siren. It was the fire department announcing the time, twelve noon, lunchtime and, more importantly for him, time to leave that life behind and seek a new path.

Who Turned off the Lights?

His older siblings were working in factories in the San Pedro Industrial Free Zone. His mother was selling food to the workers. Maiky was growing up and developing an interest in sports, but baseball wasn't in his plans.

He practiced boxing for a short time.

One night, during a boxing match in the Pepe Mallén Coliseum, his opponent punched him in the nose, turning the entire world into a huge blackout. Maiky fell and, even though there were very bright lights, he saw nothing; his whole world was dark. He woke up surprised and half-dazed, as if asking "Who turned off the lights?" That night his love for boxing was left behind in the dark tunnel from which he returned to the light.

In July 1982, something terrible happened in the Dominican Republic.

President Antonio Guzmán shot himself in the head in a bathroom of his presidential office and died. By mid-August, Salvador Jorge Blanco was sworn in as president, after winning the elections held the previous May 16.

That year Maiky started to pay serious attention to baseball. Luis, his older brother, invested his teen years playing baseball in Consuelo. He waited for the scout who never showed up at his house because, as his friends put it, "he was too small." Luis saw Maiky play ball one day and concluded that his brother had the talent and height to seduce a scout. He put him in touch with his friend, the trainer Héctor Peguero Sterling. From then on, Maiky spent a good deal of his day in the Play de Barrio Mexico, a few blocks behind his home.

While he was becoming a baseball player, Latin Americans were receiving the highest distinction in the Majors. In the eighties, two Latin American players rose to the Hall of Fame in Cooperstown.

In 1983, Juan Antonio Marichal Sánchez, became the first living Latin American player to enter the Hall of Fame. He had six seasons with twenty or more wins and a lifetime ERA of 2.89. He won 243 games, losing 142, during his successful career. He pitched a no-hit game against the Houston Astros in 1963, and was chosen to play in ten All Star Games. He pitched 244 complete games and struck out 2,303 batters. A decade earlier, in 1973, Puerto Rican Roberto Clemente was inducted into the Hall of Fame in a posthumous recognition of his career. Clemente died in a plane crash while trying to take humanitarian aid to the victims of an earthquake that destroyed the Nicaraguan capital, Managua, in 1972.

Venezuelan Luis Aparicio was inducted in the Hall of Fame in 1984. That year, baseball was played for the first time in the Olympics and, on the American team, the son of a California dentist named Mark McGwire was a shining star. After the Olympics, he became a professional player and entered the training camp of the Oakland Athletics.

During that time, there was a night when Maiky could not fall asleep, and it was not because of the mosquitoes. The cars traveling in front and beside his home were noisier than ever, as was the music in the whorehouses. He was restless. The following day he was going to a tryout for a scout from the Philadelphia Phillies. He felt he was on the brink of realizing his dreams. That thought did not let him fall asleep.

The following day the scout came, put him through a tryout, and they agreed on a contract. That day, Carlos and

Mireya did not fight because they had only reasons to celebrate.

Maiky would finally go to the United States, and that was the most important part of the whole deal. If he failed in his baseball career, he would stay in the U.S., get a job and legalize his situation just as many others had done before him.

The family kept waiting for the contract and the money that never made it into their hands. The scout never returned. All their dreams were flushed down the broken drainage system under construction across from their home. All their happiness disappeared. According to Dominican popular philosophy, happiness in the house of a poor person doesn't last as long as a cockroach in a chicken coop.

The first try did not work out; maybe it would work out some other time.

There is no one so poor who cannot find a stick straight enough to be used as a bat. There is no one so poor who cannot find old socks to make a ball. Baseball, for the Dominican poor, has kept its promise to change the life of those with the skills, discipline, devotion, and the drive to succeed.

Archivos Dominicanos

Bottom of the Seventh

Family Welfare

The best answer to anything that looks like a defeat is to not let it get you down, and that was what Maiky's family did. After being stood up by the Phillies' scout, they assumed sacrifice, an important part of baseball's philosophy, as a central part of their lifestyle. They activated the most effective program of social and human assistance ever known: the family welfare system.

Every member of the family made small sacrifices to help Maiky advance. Voluntarily, each one reduced even more their meager food rations to give him a bigger one. They gave up as much as they could in his favor. He always had the best meal, more meat than anyone else, and no one, including his stepfather, protested. Maiky became like the family piggy bank, where everyone deposited all that they had: best wishes.

He embodied the hope of his entire family.

As a young teenager, his life consisted of going about his job in one of the Industrial Free Zone factories and his baseball practices. The owner of the factory gave him his first baseball glove and put him on a flexible schedule for him to attend practices and other baseball-related commitments.

He knew that baseball was his way out, and he started taking care of himself. He exercised regularly, ate as much healthy food as he could, and withdrew from all the late night fun. One year later, when he turned 17, Maiky was a skilled power hitter; stood 5'10" tall, had almost 150 pounds of muscle, had good speed, a strong right arm and a sharp eye. Luis and Héctor were sure they had a good cock for the fight. They only waited for the opportunity to prove it.

His condition began to attract attention in the Dominican baseball community. By word of mouth, the Toronto Blue Jays invited him to their training camp. The word spread, reaching Amado Dinzey, a Texas Rangers' scout in the Dominican Republic. He got in touch with Omar Minaya, who was then a coach on one of the Rangers' minor league teams. Minaya took advantage of the opportunity to spend a weekend on the beaches of Puerto Plata and summoned the prospect for a tryout.

The bus ride between Santo Domingo and Puerto Plata is about four hours. During those 240 minutes, Maiky's nerves had him jumping, but by the time the tryout started, he had them under control.

His performance was remarkable.

The negotiations began. Minaya offered $3,000 as a bonus for signing the contract, Maiky asked for $4,000. They split the difference, and closed the deal for $3,500. Samuel Peralta (Sammy) Sosa signed with the Texas Rangers on July 30th,1985; that same year Alfredo Griffin, playing with the Oakland Athletics, won a Golden Glove in the American League.

Maiky took the money and, at age seventeen, bought himself his first bike. He shared a few bucks with his neighbors in the abandoned building where his family lived and gave the rest to his mother. The approximately $3,000 that the family got, calculated at the 8: 1 exchange rate of the time, was around 24,000 in Dominican pesos. At the time, that was a lot more than the salary of one year for a Dominican army general, and as much as the salary of a government minister.

The family's sacrifice paid off in a short time.

They remained in the old building when Maiky departed for the United States. Though they had not yet won the war against poverty, they had won an important battle. Maiky was getting ready to enter a new environment. But by then, strange things were going on in baseball.

Turning Around in the Air

The runner was about to make it to home plate, the strong arm of the right fielder threatened to cut him down. The ball and the runner traveled at almost the same speed in a tight race. The runner started what seemed to be a foot slide, but while in the air he turned around and fell face down, not half-seated, nor lying on his back, the way it was supposed to be.

That fellow was not making a fool of himself.

And he was not the only one acting out. Many runners changed their style of sliding while others did not even bother to show up to the games.

Weird things were going on in baseball.

Then rumors spread. The fans were mouthing, whispering, and gossiping about the game and the players; and something that was known but not yet accepted publicly, was openly acknowledged: drugs had invaded baseball. The change in the sliding styles of many players was driven by their need to protect a vial with cocaine in their back pocket; they started sliding headfirst to avoid losing their next fix. They changed playing technique to adapt it to their new habits.

Dominicans were also part of that chapter in the history of baseball. Pascual *—Cutá—* Pérez, a young, successful pitcher with a bright future ahead, was the most publicized victim in the Dominican Republic. His career was trashed. Cocaine hastened the deterioration of the tarnished public image that ball players had since 1976. That year César Cedeño, the Houston Astros' "Super Baby", checked into a hotel room with a woman. Some shots were heard, he got out alive, and she was dead. Publicly, what happened was never explained. Ever since, he has lived in the U.S., never returning to the Dominican Republic.

Baseball's money caused more harm than good in some lives. The XII Central American and Caribbean Games were held in the Dominican Republic in 1974 and it was defined as a "shared commitment" of the whole country. The host country received one silver medal in baseball, thanks to the remarkable performance of another player from Consuelo: Alberto Louis. At the end of the games, his professional career started. When they called him up to the Majors in 1978, everyone knew that he was a great player and expected great things from him. After one of his all night parties, he was driving while intoxicated and crashed into a moving train pulling a string of wagons loaded with sugar cane. Many of the people who were in his pickup truck died. Louis survived, but his career was put to rest in peace under the railroad tracks at the entrance of Consuelo's cemetery.

A Whole New World

In the Minor League environment which Maiky was about to enter, Dominicans and other Latin Americans faced many difficulties. Besides the language barrier, certain behaviors turned out to be important and often became stigmas. Many newcomers were just not used to a bathroom with running water. When they got to the training camp, they even found two faucets in the sinks and showers. Down home they had none, here they found two and they needed to make a choice that many times had bad consequences.

They were terribly confused.

Some interpreted the letter "C" on the cold water faucet for the Spanish word Caliente, which means hot. Trying to avoid hot water, they opened the other one, getting unpleasant boiling surprises. In the training camps, Dominicans were known for reasons other than their baseball skills.

Anyone who goes into a toilet stall and finds used toilet paper on the floor thinks "a Dominican rookie was here." In their home country, the people who have toilets with running water use a waste paper basket to put the used toilet paper in to avoid clogging the pipes. In the U.S., a wider pipe is used and paper is thrown into the bowl without fear of clogging it. Recent Dominican immigrants do not know that. Many who have lived for years in this country still do not understand the difference.

Dominicans also are famous for the unconventional things they may do when they are under pressure or think they are about to be kicked off the team. A real life story illustrates this. During a game held in 1988 in Sarasota,

Florida, in the bottom of the tenth, the game was tight and the winning run was on third base. The pitcher, a Dominican rookie, threw the ball straight into the ground. It bounced over the catcher, and the runner on third base scored to end the game.

That is exactly what he was looking for.

He hurried to the bathroom, took a shower, changed clothes and ran away. He was convinced that soon he was going to be called to the office to be informed of his dismissal. To avoid being taken by surprise, he had bought a plane ticket to New York City. He threw the ball to the ground to end the game, not caring if his team lost. If he let the game go longer, he would have missed his flight to New York City and, probably, in the morning, would be fired and forced to take a plane back to Santo Domingo.

It has happened to many players.

They are called to the office to be informed that, regrettably, due to their poor performance, the team had no choice but to let them go. They are given a ticket and someone escorts them to the plane to prevent them from staying in the country. Many players deserted training camps, afraid that they could be suddenly dismissed and sent back home. Instead of being fired, they would rather run away in order to have the opportunity to stay in the country and start a new life. This was the environment that Sammy Sosa entered in 1986.

That same year Mark McGwire debuted in the Majors during a game in Yankee Stadium.

He went 0-3.

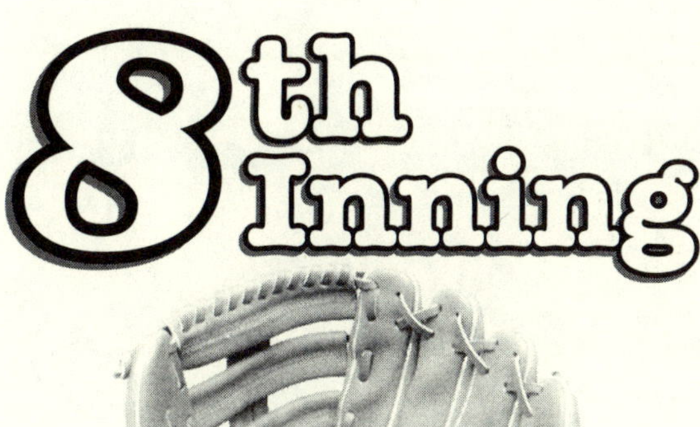
8th Inning

Top of the Eighth

The Long and Winding Road

In 1986, at age 80 and blind, Balaguer returned to the Dominican presidency and started a trial against Salvador Jorge Blanco, the president who had just left office. The former president was convicted under corruption charges and sentenced to 20 years in prison. He is the first politician in the country to end up in jail after serving in the highest Dominican office.

That same year Sammy saw and boarded a plane for the first time in his life, at age 18, and flew to Sarasota, Florida, to begin spring training. He was enchanted with the baseball diamond. It was perfect, neat and clean, fanning out as a rainbow of possibilities with a perfection he had only seen on TV. During his first days in the U.S. he felt like Alice in Wonderland.

The United States came out of his dreams to inhabit his reality and transform his whole life into a living dream. Things that existed only in fairy tales or those he had heard by word of mouth were now right in front of him. The world of those stories and movie scenes were all there, before his eyes, within his reach, under his feet.

Everything was fascinating and enveloping. The language barrier, the first brick wall that the Marichal and Rojas Alou generation faced, was still a headache for Dominican players. When Sammy arrived, there were Puerto Rican and Dominican players in the training camps. However, these did not eliminate his language problems, they just reduced them. At the end of his first season in Sarasota, his numbers were promising; playing in 61 games his average was .275. In 229 at bats he had 63 hits, 4 home runs, 28 RBIs and 11 stolen bases. His 19 doubles that year set a new record for a rookie in that league.

From the beginning, Sammy showed his gratitude for the opportunity life was giving him and decided to take full advantage of it. Thousands of Dominicans had the same opportunity and ended up with nothing. Sending a couple of dollars home and saving enough for survival with his approximately $1,000 monthly income limited his freedom of movement and kept him from getting into trouble.

The Perfect Unknown

By 1987, all baseball fans had their attention on Jorge Bell who, while playing with the Toronto Blue Jays, collected 47 homers and 134 RBIs. The attention not being paid to Bell was given to Mark McGwire. He played in 151 games with 49 homers, and was chosen Rookie of the Year. Bell was the American League MVP, becoming the first Dominican to achieve that recognition.

No one noticed it, but in 1987 Sammy, an unknown player, was transferred to Gastonia, North Carolina. This was the second city and second state in which he had played and lived in his two years in the United States. His performance improved, and he had a very good season. He played in 153 games, increased his average to .279 and doubled almost all the numbers he had the previous season. His homers hopped from four to eleven, his RBIs from 28 to 59. Some very unflattering numbers also rose: his strikeouts skyrocketed from 51 to 123.

He did not establish any new records but managed to keep the league's attention focused on him during the season. He flew to visit with his sister, Magaly, then living in The Bronx, N.Y., where his two daughters would be born years later. He then went to the Dominican Republic and played with the Leones del Escogido, the team that won the national baseball championship that year.

The Caribbean World Series was held in Santo Domingo that year and the Leones were the Dominican representative. Manager Phil Regan did not let Sammy play, he was confined to the bench.

In February 1988, he traveled to Port Charlotte, Florida, for his third year in the minors. At the end of the season, Sammy had 12 triples, establishing a new record in that league. His average plunged to .229 in 131 games with 42 stolen bases, only 9 homers and 51 RBIs.

It was already clear that his speed, strong arm and batting power were enough to take him far, if he could only put them all together. In 1988, he struck out 106 times, demonstrating that he swung at anything that moved between the mound and the batter's box. He knew that only by fanning at the balls could he increase his numbers, and that was the only way to advance his career.

The Rollercoaster Ride

Perhaps coincidence does not exist; it may only be a word to define things we do not understand. It may very well be a synonym for ignorance. The instability that his family experienced while living on the road probably trained Sammy for a test that could have been a lot harder on him. Besides dealing with the language problems, different food, adapting to a new life and fighting to improve his numbers, 1989 was unstable for him. That year, before he was 21, he had played in six cities, two countries and four leagues, not including the Dominican Republic. In 1989 his dreams became a beautiful reality, to then crash down in an awful and unstable nightmare.

He started the 1989 season in Tulsa, Oklahoma; the Rangers having promoted him to Double A. He played in 66 games with an average of .297. He reduced his strikeouts from 106 in the previous season to 52. He had fewer errors and seemed to be a little more patient with the bat, being less desperate in the batter's box.

By mid-June, the manager gave him the news.

The Rangers had an opening in its Major League right field and, as he turned 21, Sammy was called up from Double A, skipping Triple A completely. It was as if he were promoted from fourth to sixth grade, without completing the fifth.

On June 16, 1989, at Yankee Stadium, Sammy took his first turn at bat in the Majors and got a hit against Andy Hawkins. Five days later, he faced a living legend of the mound —Roger Clemens— and got his first home run in the Big Show, as an announcement of what was to come.

The Major Leagues were a new and difficult environment for him, but fate was on his side. His countryman and fellow villager, Julio Franco, was among the Rangers' stars and gave him all the support and orientation he could. After 25 games, Sammy had a very weak .238 average, his strikeouts were in a dead heat: 20 hits and 20 strikeouts. After rising very high, it was his turn to live the other side, to experience gravity.

He crashed.

The manager told him he was to be returned to the minors, to a Triple A team in Oklahoma City. There he played in only ten games. On July 29, the manager gave him more news: he needed to leave Oklahoma City and the United States. He was being traded to the Chicago White Sox. They sent him to their Triple A team in Vancouver, British Columbia, Canada. There, he had a .367 average and struck out only seven times.

He demonstrated more control of the bat. Less than a month later, on August 22nd, the White Sox manager informed him of his new destiny and gave him a plane ticket. He was flying to Chicago, returning to the Majors. He played in 22 games and, just as he did in his first year, his strikeouts and hits were even. He had a .273 average, playing in 99 games, with 27 hits and 27 strikeouts.

For Sammy the whole year of 1989 was a non-stop roller-coaster ride. He went up, came back down, turned and kept on going straight ahead. He finished the season dizzy and disoriented. The only thing he was sure of was: he did not know if he had secured his job for the next season. He went back to the Dominican Republic to play in the country's winter championship.

He took the time to do something that became a ritual for him. He gave money to his former colleagues from the Parque Duarte, giving up to $300 in Dominican currency to his fellow shoe shiners, dish washers, and fruit peddlers. All those with whom he had shared the last years of his childhood in the park, and many of the homeless with whom he shared the old building across from the Estadio Tetelo Vargas, got some cash from him.

Between 1986 and 1989, while Sammy was in the minors, Latin American players won nine Golden Gloves; Dominican Tony —*Cabeza*— Fernández won four of them.

Will This Ever Stop?

By 1990, the White Sox considered Sammy a mature player with an excellent command of the so-called Five Tools of the game. He had remarkable batting skills, speed, a strong arm, very good defensive skills and overall power. They opened a place for him in the Majors. He played in 153 games, struck out 150 times, and ended the season with an anemic .233 average. This was his first complete season in the majors and his numbers were still depressing.

At the end of that season, he returned to the Dominican Republic to play and built his family's first house behind the old building where they lived until then. Barrio México is one of San Pedro's slums, and he built the home in the poorest section of this barrio, called Jarro Sucio which means "dirty can."

The following year he started the season in Canada. The White Sox sent him down to Triple A. Again. He played 32 games, struck out 32 times, got 31 hits, and his average was .267. He ended the season in the Majors, playing 116 games: 64 hits, 10 doubles, 10 homers, 33 RBIs and 13 stolen bases.

The decade of the 90s started well for Latin American players in the Major Leagues: In 1991, Panamanian Rod Carew was the fourth Latin American to enter the Hall of Fame in Cooperstown. For his career he had 3,053 hits. He was the batting champion seven times with a lifetime average of .328. He was chosen Rookie of the Year in the American League in 1967 and 10 years later MVP. He was named to the All Star Game 17 times.

That same year Julio Franco achieved an average of .341, becoming the batting champion for the American League. He was the third Dominican with that distinction.

At the end of 1991, Sammy had an average of .203, but his situation with the White Sox was uglier than his numbers. He had an awful reputation and an even worse interpersonal and professional relationship with the batting coach. Among team members, there was the perception that he was a selfish guy with no discipline. He was accused of looking out only for himself with total disregard for the team. That was a terrible thing to say about someone who is supposed to be a teamplayer. It suggested that he had a personality that was totally contrary to the very spirit of baseball.

The following year the two teams in Chicago exchanged players.

Jorge Bell was traded from the Cubs to the White Sox in exchange for the pitcher Ken Patterson and Sammy. Then, expressing his satisfaction after getting away from the White Sox, Sammy said that he felt as if he had just "*gotten out of jail.*"

In Chicago, the White Sox and the Cubs have the same relationship as the Yankees and the Mets in New York, as Licey and Escogido in Santo Domingo. They are eternal rivals, competing for the hearts of their city's fans. And their fight is tough. The White Sox were glad to get rid of Sammy, and he felt the same way. Both were happy. It was like a divorce where the couple is in agreement, with separation producing as much pleasure as the honeymoon once did.

Polín Jiménez

The four Dominican Batting Champions, from the top left, Mateo Rojas Alou, Ricardo Carty, Julio Franco and Alex Rodríguez. Carty and Franco are both from Consuelo.

The Perfect Combination

Sammy exited the White Sox chased by an awful reputation.

They said he was:

Deaf: he did not listen to the coaches.

Arrogant: he thought he knew everything.

Selfish: he thought only about his own numbers, not the team's goals.

Sick with gold fever: he only cared about money.

After hearing these things over and over, even he may have ended up believing them. Probably some of them were true. So much negativity could not have come only from those who run the White Sox. That is a baseball team, not a bunch of creative geniuses. Sammy became many of those negative pictures painted about him or, at least, he thought them to be true and, for all intents and purposes, the outcome was the same.

Just across town, in another section of Chicago, Sammy was perceived in a complete different way.

For the Cubs he was:

An individual with great natural abilities: he only needed the proper orientation.

Very talented, but unaware of elementary rules and tricks of the game.

Ready to learn, if only they could find the right way to teach him.

Arrogant, only because he thought that humility would make him vulnerable.

The Cubs started to emphasize the positive things they saw in him, those the White Sox critics never let him see. The Cubs accepted him as the new little cub in the pack, gave him security, nourishment and helped him grow.

In his personal life something very important happened.

When he got to the Cubs, he was a new man trying to summon the best he could find in himself. He was interested in being the best person he could be. He loved everyone and felt that the whole world loved him. He was a man head over heels in love, trying to do all that he possibly could to deserve the love of his new mate: a beautiful Dominican TV model.

Sonia was the best thing that ever happened to him and, indeed, his only source of stability during those uncertain years when he changed teams, cities, countries and leagues. He met her in 1991, when he did not know if he was in the Majors or the Minors, if he was coming or going, rising or falling. She gave him emotional support. The Cubs gave him new professional horizons. At home and at work, everyone was re-affirming his positive qualities. He felt fortunate in the game and in love. If his departure from the White Sox was a step ahead, meeting Sonia and getting to the Cubs completed what he needed to send his self-esteem all the way up to the sky. He was now living the ideal situation; conditions were well suited for him to perform his best. And he did it.

Life was smiling upon him. Finally.

The Mountain Top

In 1992, Jorge Bell had 25 home runs and 111 RBIs.

There was no doubt that the White Sox had made a good deal with the player exchange. The Cubs could not say exactly the same; but they kept their faith in Sammy's future alive, and his performance improved at an incredibly fast pace. Between May 31st and June the 10th, he hit four homers with many RBIs. Everything was beginning to shine when, the sky above him "turned dark and full of clouds."

Disaster struck.

During a game with the Montreal Expos, pitcher Dennis Martínez threw an inside pitch and Sammy could not get out of the way on time. The ball did not hit the bat but his right hand, and some bones were broken. Between June 13th and 27th, he was on the disabled list.

In July, he returned with an even better performance.

In nine games he got nine hits, three homers and nine RBIs. His average was .385, and the Cubs management's faith in their new prospect was reaffirmed. They began to see that the deal made with the White Sox was, indeed, a good one.

Again, all that changed in another confusing second.

Sammy swung at a pitch; the bat barely touched the ball, which got tangled up between his feet. He tumbled out of the batter's box. He was rushed to the hospital; the X rays revealed a broken left ankle. He could not play for the rest of the season. In 67 games he had 68 hits, 8 homers and 25 RBIs.

In 1993, his ascent to the mountaintop began.

On July 2nd he got six hits in one game against Colorado. On September 29th, against the L.A. Dodgers, he stole four bases in the same game. These were only parts of his outstanding performance during the year.

He totaled 156 hits, 25 doubles, 5 triples, 33 homers, 93 RBIs and he stole 36 bases. And he became the first player in the history of the Cubs to hit more than 30 home runs and steal more than 30 bases in the same season.

Chasing trucks loaded with sugar cane and the hours spent chewing and playing around with it were beginning to produce awesome results. He was an extraordinarily fast runner because of a simple reason: since birth, he was hunted by poverty. After 28 years of running away from starvation, Sammy won the race.

His remarkable vision can also be explained by his poverty years. From an early age, he played with almost invisible balls, made out of old socks. Then he used old baseballs that had lost their plain white color and were stained and confusing to the eyes as a soldier dressed in camouflage in the middle of the forest. He learned to identify and time an almost invisible object, so it was very easy for him to see the plain white ball with its red stitches that pitchers threw at him in the Major Leagues. He sees them with more clarity than other players.

When he became "Mr. 30 x 30," he had lived two years with Sonia; Kenia, his oldest daughter was born during his first year with the Cubs. That was a spectacular season for him. He was winning the war against poverty with his bat, and he proclaimed it in a unique way.

At the end of the season, he went back to San Pedro with something big. It was not a necklace, not even a big one, it was something slightly smaller than a license plate, made out of gold and diamonds. More than a piece of jewelry, it looked like a large print multiplication tool for students with limited vision. It said: "30 x 30". The symbol in the middle was made out of two small bats carved in gold. The numbers, also in gold, had diamonds in them.

In San Pedro, he shared money with his old buddies and friends, he went to the shoreline avenue, known as Malecón. There he sat on the hood of one of his cars, bare chested, exhibiting his necklace as a personal symbol. That year he made himself a very humble and significant gift. He made a deal with another Cubs player, changing his number from 25 to 21, the number of his hero, Puerto Rican Roberto Clemente. Now Sammy was "Mr. 30 x 30," and that gave him some privileges, among which was to choose the number he wanted.

Higher, Even Higher

Ballplayers walked out after voting to strike, during the 1994 season, after only 105 games were played. Sammy had a .300 average, with 128 hits, 17 doubles, 6 triples, 25 homers, 70 RBIs, and 22 stolen bases. If it weren't for the strike, it is probable that he would have ended up being the first player in the history of the game with three straight seasons in the "30 x 30" club. The Cubs rewarded him with a $4 million contract for the following season. That was the highest salary he had earned up to that point. The new contract was a definite insurance policy against poverty.

In 1994, two very important things happened to Dominican players in the Majors. Felipe Rojas Alou was appointed manager of the Montreal Expos, becoming the first Dominican to manage a team in the Big Show. At the end of the season, he was chosen Manager of the Year, and Raúl Mondesí became the second Dominican chosen Rookie of the Year.

When Sammy returned to San Pedro, he bought his

mom another house and had extensive remodeling done. In the Parque Duarte, as usual, he gave away money and clothes to his old buddies and returned to the U.S. for the upcoming season.

He earned every penny of that year's contract.

He was chosen the National League Player of the Week on two occasions. Until then, no Cubs player had won the distinction twice in the same season. Sammy closed that season with 151 hits, 17 doubles, 36 homers, 119 RBIs, and 34 stolen bases. At the end, *The Sporting News* chose him for their All Star Team. His stardom had transcended his team by far.

By 1996 he got a new contract: $10 million for two years. During that season, as in many others, the Cubs were having a very hard time, but Sammy was doing just fine. He became the soul and hope of the team. Yes, the same guy who left the White Sox with the reputation of being selfish and arrogant was now the one who carried the team on his shoulders. He was chosen Player of the Week many times by his own team and also by independent news and sports organizations.

Sammy became the first Cubs player to hit two homers in the same inning, but few noticed in Santo Domingo. The same day of his accomplishment, May 16, 1996, Dominicans flooded the voting booths to cast their ballots in the national election. For the first time in 30 years, Balaguer was not a candidate to become president. The country was starting out with a new Constitution that was basically written to prevent him from running. A new electoral system was being used for the first time, according to which, candidates needed a minimum of 51 percent of the vote to get into office. Neither Leonel Fernández, nor Peña Gómez, the two front runners, got the required votes to win.

The runoff election followed.

Peña Gómez had strong political support from Jorge Blanco, the man who Balaguer sent to jail; if he won the elections, revenge against the old leader would be sure. Despite being blind, Balaguer could clearly see that he was in danger. He decided to save his own skin while paying an old favor owed Juan Bosch for having returned from exile to legalize his election in 1966. Balaguer called his supporters to cast votes for Fernández, Bosch's party's candidate, to prevent Peña Gómez from winning the elections.

On June 5th, three weeks after the elections, Sammy connected three home runs in the same game and his numbers kept soaring. By August 20th, he already had 40 home runs and 99 RBIs. During a game at Wrigley Field, Sammy was at bat with the bases loaded when he got hit with a pitch that broke his right hand. In this painful situation, he was credited with his 100th RBI. He remained on the disabled list for the rest of the season.

Returning to San Pedro, he repeated his ritual of distributing money and clothes among buddies and relatives. While recovering from his broken hand, he invested $2.8 million to build his "Plaza 30 x 30," a small, three-floor shopping center with many retail spaces. In the entrance of the building, there is a little fountain with a small sculpture of someone batting and a sign stating that money dropped in would benefit children who shine shoes and live on the streets. He made donations to schools and several other non-profit organizations in his hometown and other places in the Dominican Republic.

When he returned to Chicago for the 1997 season, rumors spread that he was negotiating to leave the Cubs. The reality was that it made a lot of sense for anyone to try to get him off that team. They were far from winning anything, and they seemed to be a brother team with San Pedro's Estrellas Orientales. The fans of both teams became mourners. They went to the stadium, not to enjoy the game or dream of a victory, but to commiserate with each other while the team suffered one defeat after another. By mid-season, before Sammy's contract expired, the Cubs strongly denied the rumors.

They announced the signing of a new four-year contract for $42.5 million. The Cubs had never paid so much money to any player.

Now Sammy was not simply a millionaire, he was a multi-millionaire; one of the richest men in the history of baseball to date.

Armed with his bat, he had defeated poverty. Forever. Neither he, nor anyone in his family would need money ever again. They had money forever and a day. The way the contract was drafted, besides a truckload of money, it included a great message for him regarding his future. He was to get in shape for the upcoming season. To deliver the performance they were expecting from him, he needed to improve his batting.

In 1997 Sammy was not the only Dominican player making big news. Alex Rodríguez became the fourth Dominican batting Champion. Mateo Rojas Alou was the first in 1966, Ricardo Carty was the second in 1970. Julio Franco was the third in 1991.

Polín Jiménez

Felipe Rojas Alou is the first Dominican to manage a Major League team. Raúl Mondesí was the second Dominican to become Rookie of the Year, and Pedro Martínez the first Dominican winner of a Cy Young Award.

9th
Inning

Top of the Ninth

The Clear Message

One dog told him so.

Long time ago.

He doesn't speak dog.

It was Lance Johnson, called "One Dog" by White Sox's sports caster Ken Harrelson, who recommended that Sammy fine tune his skills.

"Hey man, if you learn to reduce your strikeouts, to control and put more flexibility in your swing, you will get a lot more hits," Johnson told him during the years spent with the White Sox.

Every place he went, people told him the same thing. They complimented his natural talents but insisted he needed education to get them under control in order to better benefit from them.

The message was everywhere.

The $42.2 million contract he signed was as juicy as a rotten tomato, and it cried it out to him in a different way. In writing. The juiciest installments, those of $11 and $12 million, were scheduled for the years 2000 and 2001. That was a bet on his future, not a payment for his present, because when he signed it in 1997, he had the lowest average in his history with the Cubs: .251. The team was betting on his future; Sammy could not lose this one. He worked as hard as he could to make the bright future that everyone saw for him become the present.

His first smart move was to accept that he was not perfect and needed to look for the best way to improve his batting habits. To understand that he could not do it alone and seek help with humility was the second one. To pay attention to his instructor, follow his recommendations, and to study and practice with devotion was the third key element in his success formula.

Sammy did not have much formal education. His childhood options were to survive or study. He is still alive. He knew, nevertheless, that studying was the way to achieve his goals. He learned that lesson from his own life story. As a kid, he had no opportunity to attend school like other children, but the classroom is a central part of all his accomplishments in the Majors.

In the Major League's classrooms, he started to develop his own potential.

Few people know it, but ballplayers attend school on a regular basis; Major League teams have schools for their players. They invest long hours studying and learning things that are necessary to survive in their new life of fame and fortune. The Major Leagues are filled with major problems, major challenges; major traps. Up there, the cost of any mistake, no matter how small, can be huge.

In those schools, ballplayers learn to manage their money. Life is difficult with no money, true enough, but this does not mean that it is easier in opulence. Players are taught how to handle, process and adapt to the sudden changes in their lives.

In the Major Leagues, players live under a constant threat of becoming tangled up in legal troubles with women. That is why they are taught self-control techniques and ways to identify traps wrapped up in lovely women's bodies; to figure out the agendas of females well-trained in blackmail, extortion and other ways of drawing money from them. There are also underage girls with woman-like bodies who have made many players fall into temptation, followed by the court-ordered fines and punitive damages.

Many players have gotten involved with underage teens or adult women who afterward accused them of rape or sexual assault. Many of them have even served jail time because of this.

Among the subjects they study in these schools, of course, are baseball's philosophy, objectives and techniques. Sammy invested long hours studying to become the fine player he is with the outstanding personal manners he displays. He knew that without his hours of studying, he would not have risen to stardom. He expanded his studies and practice to move to a higher level of professional achievement.

He Was Ready

It is widely known that when a student is ready to receive a new lesson, he or she picks out the right teacher from whom to learn it. Sammy's moment came and so did his teacher. On Friday, June 27 1997, the new contract for $42.2 million was announced. By Monday, July 14 the Cubs hired Jeff Pentland as their batting coach. Pentland is not just another batting coach. Before moving to Chicago, he was a professor at the University of California at Riverside. There he taught history, philosophy, physical education, biomechanics, golf and tennis. In baseball, he coached batting at all levels of the Minor and Major Leagues.

It was one of those things that was meant to be. The Cubs hired him when Sammy was ready to broaden his professional horizons. Pentland is a professional educator who understands the learning styles of different people and seeks the methodology that best helps his students learn.

With Sammy, he produced a precious jewel.

Pentland first overcame inner-personal barriers; he offered the respect and the space to earn Sammy's trust. There was no doubt about it, Sammy had excellent abilities and everyone knew that Pentland was a great coach. When they agreed to work together and started to practice under the bleachers of Wrigley Field, a great player met a great coach. Sammy was an eager student willing to work as hard as necessary to achieve his goal. Pentland was an experienced coach, ready to produce his masterpiece. It was one of those extraordinary combinations that produces marvelous results.

Pentland started with a rigorous evaluation.

He saw three basic skills in Sammy: talent, power and aggressiveness. He also found that something prevented Sammy from putting them together to take greater advantage of this extraordinary combination. Pentland identified the first and major obstacle: one of Sammy's most important qualities was out of control and therefore affecting him negatively. Aggressiveness is a double-edged blade: if it is controlled, it is a powerful weapon; otherwise, it is a great obstacle.

Sammy needed to learn physical and mental techniques to control his aggressiveness.

Pentland suggested to him new ways to better manage his time in the batter's box. Sammy needed to take more advantage of the fractions of seconds that a ball spends between the mound and home plate. In that nick of time, the batter decides whether or not he will swing. That is one of the most crucial moments in any sport.

Sammy is one of those batters who uses the "tap step" style in the batter's box. He begins his swing by lifting the front foot in order to create momentum before hitting the ball. But he did the "tap step" when the ball was already upon him. He needed to do it as the ball left the mound. Pentland understood that Sammy lost precious and decisive fractions of seconds because he "tap stepped" too late. Sammy's learning style was more suited to audio-visual media and practice.

At the end of the season Sammy went to the Dominican Republic loaded with videos as study materials and with specific homework to do. He would study his own batting style and that of other players, make comparisons, and arrive at his own conclusions about the changes he needed to make in order to achieve his goal. Student and instructor set the goals for the upcoming 1998, season and, even though he did not achieve them all, Sammy hit 66 home runs, which was in no way, shape or form one of their objectives.

Doing His Home Work

He returned to Santo Domingo, distributed gifts and money and devoted himself to study. He watched the videos, replayed them, reviewed them in slow motion, and learned far more than he could have imagined. The camera catches details to which we do not pay attention in normal circumstances, no matter how clear they are before our eyes. The players in the videos were Mark Grace of the Cubs, Chipper Jones of the Atlanta Braves, Bernie Williams of the New York Yankees and Sammy himself.

All of them use the "tap step" method before swinging their bats. The majority do it as the ball leaves the mound, but Sammy did it only when the ball is already upon him. For that reason he swung with his body out of balance and his power was not properly concentrated at the point when the bat meets the ball.

His homework objective was to learn to "tap step" earlier in the process. In that way he could take advantage of his movement to balance his body, distribute his weight and concentrate his strength before his bat hit the ball.

From Santo Domingo he phoned Pentland many times, engaging him in long chats, reporting his progress or seeking answers to the questions that arose in the process. Their conversations served both men in a very important way: to make sure they kept working toward the same objective with equal interest and mutual respect. Sammy spent the fall and winter semester of 1997, in the campus of the Universidad Central del Este (UCE), San Pedro's college. There were two pitchers for Sammy's batting practices, one was Abuelo, which means Grandfather in Spanish. He is the senior coach of the college's baseball team. The other was the one and only, Héctor Peguero Sterling. The three men engaged in long practices, so long that they can only be compared with the intensive training that some fighting cock owners press upon their animals before taking them to the gallera. He left all his old batting habits behind and picked up new ones in the UCE baseball diamond.

When Abuelo's arm got tired, Peguero Sterling got on the mound. The pitchers took turns, Sammy continued without tiring. He showed up at the college's diamond every day around noon and begin a marathon of batting and fielding until sunset. As darkness enveloped the UCE's baseball diamond in San Pedro, Sammy took off to Santo Domingo to study his videos. No one knows for sure how many hours he invested in front of the screen, but it is safe to estimate that he invested around 40 hours in practice every week on the college campus during the fall and winter semester.

The Wind Wept

The frozen February wind was blowing snowflakes over Wrigley Field in Chicago when Sammy arrived in Mesa, Arizona, for spring training. All the players should have reported to training camp by the twentieth of the month; he got there on the 23rd, but everyone knew he would depart right away.

An urgent emotional situation demanded his presence.

Sammy always had his own fan club.

His first fan was his brother Luis, who had first noticed Sammy's natural qualities; he was the one who "discovered" him. He signed up a customer whose shoes he had shined many times in his fan club. Bill Chase owned a factory in the town's Industrial Free Zone. The two met at the Parque Duarte in San Pedro de Macorís, and he hired Sammy as a minimum wage worker with a flexible schedule so he could practice baseball.

With the Cubs, Sammy captivated new fans and brought warmth to many hearts, or at least to enough to make the club invest $42.5 million in him. By the time he joined the Cubs, his life seemed to be coming together in a strange, but wonderful way. A lot of positive things were happening to him, including meeting one of the most important fans of his career. Admiration and respect grew between him and this special fan. As their friendship blossomed, changes began to show up in the work of this legendary sportscaster. During his 50 years in the game from behind the microphone, Harry Caray was known for his merciless criticisms of players' weak spots. He was the Cubs' official voice and one of the most authoritative voices in baseball.

When he became Sammy's fan, Caray decided to promote the positive aspects of the Dominican outfielder, transmitting them to the whole world. He was Sammy's most important admirer and protector.

The fans began to see Sammy through Caray's eyes. On February 27, 1998, a huge bash took over Santo Domingo's Malecón, the seafront boulevard, with the double celebration of the country's carnival and its Independence Day.

Sammy had flown four days earlier to Mesa, Arizona,

but he was now in Chicago. When his plane landed and he made it through the eternal crowd at O'Hare Airport, he felt the city wrapped in a bubble of silence. He heard only the wind blowing between the skyscrapers, which wasn't a new sound for him, but this time it felt different. There were no seagulls flying over the Windy City's Lake Shore Drive, and Lake Michigan's waves were motionless, suspended in the air, frozen, forming shapeless and sad ice sculptures as standing examples of the Midwest's winter blues.

There was no anger in the wind's roaring between the skyscrapers. That winter afternoon, under leafless and ice covered trees, Caray was buried in a Chicago cemetery.

And Sammy felt as if the wind were weeping.

Bottom of the Ninth

Holy Cow!

Long before Felipe Rojas Alou moved up to the Majors and before Padre José lived in Consuelo, Caray was narrating baseball. He meant as much to American fans, as Argentinean Buck Canel, Ecuadorian Jaime Jarrín, and Dominican Billy Berroa meant to Latin American fans. Caray's voice transmitted images and emotions to millions of fans for two whole generations; he was one of those sportscasters who literally made the fans "see with their ears."

February 14, 1998, was the 30th anniversary of the Estrellas Orientales' last victory in the Dominican baseball championship. That day, Caray suffered a massive heart attack and was rushed to the hospital.

He passed away four days later.

No one else directed the fans' choir during the seventh inning stretch and the singing of the baseball song "Take Me Out To the Ball Game" like he did. The fans felt the emptiness that his death left behind and, for Sammy, the void was even deeper. Caray's death helped him appreciate the close spiritual relationship between men. There was a kind of mysterious dance between them, and this was another part of the enchantment of the 1998 season.

Caray was one of Sammy's best fans, but he wouldn't see him implement his new batting techniques. His spirit, nevertheless, was always present. Sammy started out dedicating his performance during the season to his deceased friend. That was not a simple declaration for promotional purposes, it was ratified 66 times. After each homer, when Sammy brings his fingers to his chest forming the "V" of victory, he does so in memory of Caray, proclaiming the triumph of friendship over death.

Rumors spread very quickly.

It was said that the ghost of Caray was protecting Sammy and, for many people, something that happened on June 5, before the Home Run Derby, served as a confirmation. Jim Parque, the White Sox left-hander, was on the mound at Wrigley Field; it was the fifth inning. Sammy had one ball and two strikes; there was a man on base. He swung at the fourth pitch and sent the ball on a 370 foot-trip between right and centerfield. That was his 17th homer of the season, but no one paid attention to it. That very day the fan's focus was centered on Busch Stadium of the Saint Louis' Cardinals. With the same count as Sammy and with a man on base, Mark McGwire hit his 28th home run.

That was the sporting news of the day.

Less attention was paid to what happened at Wrigley Field with the game tied in the eighth inning. Magglio Ordóñez of the White Sox hit a line drive between right and center and the ball hit the fence, but it did not bounce. It stayed wrapped up in the vines that cover the Wrigley Field fence. The rules of the game are clear; it was a double; Sammy advanced quietly and cleared the vine as he took out the ball and threw it back to the infield.

That ball, in the eyes of many fans, was a kind of mysterious message sent by Caray covering Sammy with special powers that everyone would later see. The rumor gained strength and sounded over the radio and TV waves in Chicago. At the end of June, he had set a new record in baseball.

Sammy hit 20 home runs in one month.

No one had ever done that. He ended June with 33 homers, while McGwire had 37. Only four homers were the difference, but on a national level no one paid any attention to Sammy because Ken Griffey Jr., with 33 home runs, was the player in competition with McGwire.

Sammy started to attract attention to himself in a very slow and gentle way, suavemente (softly), as the lyrics of an Elvis Crespo's song goes. By mid-July, McGwire had 42 home runs and Griffey Jr. 39 Sammy was behind with 36, and on a national level, that wasn't a big deal.

In Chicago, the fans missed Caray for other reasons besides singing the baseball song. The legendary sportscaster had a peculiar form of calling the home runs. Every time Sammy hit one, the fans, convinced that Caray was protecting him, basically "heard" his voice from the afterlife, celebrating each home run. By the end of July, there had been 42 occasions on which they may have "heard" Caray celebrating Sammy's home runs. With each homer, the slugger performed his ritual in memory of his friend.

Now the public believed that Sammy was protected by Caray's ghost. That was the only way to explain his extraordinary performance. Sammy was hitting two and even three homers in a single game, and sometimes in the same inning. Every time he stood in the batter's box, he scared the pitchers and drove the fans crazy. Between July 27 and 28 he hit three homers, two of them with the bases loaded: two Grand Slams. Those things happen only in baseball fantasies.

And Sammy became a synonym for the phrase that Caray coined for the homers: "Holy Cow."

Secret Weapons

The rumor that he was protected by Caray's ghost covered Sammy with a mysterious and invisible aura. Behind this transparent curtain, in front of the fans, he became another player, but no one noticed it. He was not as desperate as he was before when he used to swing at anything that crossed the plate.

The new Sammy was not fighting to control the ball, but to control himself. And he did it. He was a pretty cool and quiet fellow, very patient, mature and selective. He learned to stay "behind" the ball and, when he swung his bat, he did so with all his body perfectly balanced with his power concentrated over more flexible hips.

In all reality, he was another person, one who had recently come out of the UCE's campus in San Pedro. This new fellow was wrapped up in Sammy's body and had the same number 21, which confused the heck out of many pitchers. They kept throwing the same pitches with which they successfully struck him out in the past. They didn't know Sammy had managed to turn his past weakness into an arsenal of powerful, new secret weapons.

The Spirit Of Baseball

By July's end, the competition between McGwire and Griffey Jr. was baseball's top news. Both players, nevertheless, proved to be incapable of handling the attention and couldn't manage the stress as gracefully as the fans expected. McGwire said that, due to the pressure from the media and the fans, he felt like a "caged bird." Griffey Jr. was far more direct: he told reporters that he had no intentions of answering any questions or talking about his homers. In July, Griffey Jr. moved down to third place as Sammy moved up to the second spot with 42 homers, behind McGwire's 45.

Then Sammy became a counselor.

The home run pressure made Roger Maris lose his hair 37 years ago; the same stress was melting down McGwire and Griffey Jr. in 1998. Sammy, meanwhile, took it on and managed to stay as cool as cool can be. He handled it as the most fun of all games. He defined the experience as grand and fun; he said that there was no reason to be worried or nervous, and reminded everyone that baseball was nothing but a game, and that it should be viewed as such.

He was always open to answer reporters' questions and never opened his mouth without praising the game, the fans, and the U.S. In his press conferences, it was routine to listen to jokes from his lips and words loaded with honest and innocent expressions. It was as if he were letting out, before the whole country, through the media, the childlike personality he had to suppress during his hard life in San Pedro de Macorís. He was being the child he never was. On the baseball field, a series of small gestures brought him closer and closer to the fans. Every time he had the opportunity in batting practice or during the game, he gave away balls to the fans.

Those expressions of sincere childlike ingenuity helped baseball to recover part of its innocence, lost almost 25 years earlier. Meanwhile, August came, and it was clear that Griffey Jr. was out of the race, as he stayed behind McGwire and Sammy.

Then Sammy surprised the world with a great declaration of sportsmanship. He took on the job of praising the first baseman from the Cardinals and predicted that McGwire would be the man to break the record and that he, Sammy, was only there to push him to achieve the goal.

Something very strange happened.

The majority of the fans were pushing for Sammy to break the home run records, while Sammy himself was publicly pushing for McGwire to do it. He repeated, over and over, that his goal was to stimulate McGwire to hit more homers and help the Cubs to make it to the playoffs. His performance on and off the field, and his willingness to sacrifice himself for the benefit of his team, brought back to baseball part of its lost magic.

He opened a window through which the fans came to see players as good guys, as in previous generations, willing to sacrifice themselves for the team's welfare. Ballplayers became nice fellows again, like those heroes of yesterdays, willing to sacrifice themselves as part of their ritual journey toward a collective success. The benefit of their community of players was their main goal. McGwire was ahead most of the time when it came to connecting homers, but Sammy controlled the human side of the derby to the very end. Besides reuniting players and fans, he became a real star of the game. Sammy was the one who brought baseball back to its very essence: to entertain the country in a positive and healthy way. His performance made the fans feel proud of the extraordinary achievement of a fellow man, a member of the human family.

On August 10, Sammy hit two home runs at 3 Com Park in San Francisco, playing against the Giants. In that game, he tied McGwire with his 46th homer. The following day the first baseman of the Cardinals hit number 47, and on August 16 Sammy blasted his 47th.

That was a very special homer for many people.

The Dominican Republic is the only country in the Americas, and perhaps the world, with two independence days, and August 16th is the second and final one. That is the official day for presidential inaugurations and President Leonel Fernández was celebrating his second year in office. That night, the president and the slugger exchanged congratulations in a phone conversation. With that night's homer, Sammy may have evoked one last smile from President Clinton. The following day he was to be deposed before a Grand Jury. There he would have to answer questions about his sexual intimacy as part of a scandal that threatened to evict him from the White House.

The Home Run Derby was, in fact, one of the only positive things going on in those days, not only for Clinton, but for the whole country. It became the best and most neutral instrument of political distraction ever found; it was like a gift from the Gods for a country on the edge of political and moral bankruptcy. Three days later, Wrigley Field became the scene of one of the most emotional games in baseball history. The Cardinals were visiting and in the fifth inning. With two outs and one man on base, right-handed Kent Bottenfield threw Sammy a fast ball that flew over the fence between left and center field, his 48th homer, and with it he passed McGwire.

He did not lead for very long.

Three innings later, in the eighth, McGwire was at bat with three balls and a strike. He sent Matt Karchner's fifth pitch over the fence to tie with Sammy at 48 homers. The game was also tied. Extra innings were played and, in the tenth, McGwire hit his 49th to lead the derby once again. At the end of August, both players were tied with 55 homers and became the center of the world's attention.

Sammy took advantage of the opportunity to repeat that he had no intention of breaking any record, that his goal was to help his team make it to the playoffs. And he announced his willingness to trade any opportunity to break records, if it was necessary, to make sure the Cubs won the series. He proclaimed once again his devotion to self-sacrifice for the benefit of his team.

He embodied the very spirit of baseball.

La Gran Fiesta

The entire month of September is a great fiesta for Latin Americans in the United States and in their countries of origin. By September 25th, Sammy had already established new records in various categories of baseball and, for 45 minutes, he was the world home run champion. He broke most of the team records, those of the division and the league, then set out towards wider and more far-reaching marks.

It all started on Saturday September 12th while the Milwaukee Brewers were visiting Wrigley Field for a weekend doubleheader. The left-handed Valerio de los Santos had two men on base with one out in the top of the seventh inning. Sammy had a count of three balls and two strikes; the sixth pitch was a fastball that, with the same speed, flew over the fence to fall in the yard of a neighboring house. That day he became the first Latin American, Dominican and black, in the entire history of baseball, to hit 60 home runs in a single season. Before him, that level of performance was reserved for players such as Ruth, Maris, and McGwire. The runs that he batted in with that homer, contributed to the victory of the Cubs, 15 to 12, and put the team closer to making the playoffs.

The following day he hit his 61st homer off right-handed Broswell Patrick and became one of only three players to have reached that level. He left Babe Ruth behind, and now was in an exclusive club with Maris and McGwire. In the bottom of the ninth, in the same game, the Cubs had their last chance; the Brewers were ahead, 10-9. There was one out, no one on base and Sammy had a 2-1 count. He went with the fourth pitch and sent it into a 480 foot-trip over the fence, becoming the second man in history to reach 62 home runs in a single season. The game was tied, and in the bottom of the tenth, Cubs' first baseman Mark Grace hit another homer, and his team won, 11-10.

September 15th is the beginning of one of the most extraordinary events recorded in the continent's history. That day, in 1821, five Central American republics, Costa Rica, Nicaragua, Honduras, El Salvador and Guatemala, achieved their independence at the same time, without spilling a drop of blood. The celebrations continued until the following day, the 16th, which is the Mexican Independence Day.

Even in the most remote cities of the United States, that day begins Hispanic Heritage Month celebrations. Almost half of Latin America's population is celebrating independence, and, in the U.S., Hispanics are honoring their heritage. That very day Sammy and his team went to a city that even has a Spanish name: San Diego, on the border between the U.S. and Latin America. In the seventh inning of this game held at the Qualcomm Stadium, Sammy connected for a double and batted in two runs, putting the Cubs ahead of the Padres. In the bottom of that inning, the Padres tied the game and in the top of the eighth, reality became confused, once again, with fantasy. The bases were loaded, Sammy had a ball and a strike. The next pitch flew over the fence to become Sammy's 63rd homer of the season with a Grand Slam, giving the Cubs a 6-2 win.

That Wednesday, the Padres' management could not contain their own emotions and fireworks sparked under the sky, over Qualcomm Stadium. It was the only time to date that a losing home team gave a tribute of recognition to the winner, who was basically one person: Sammy scored two runs and batted in four.

That night, the fireworks lighted the skies of Mexico City, Central America and San Diego, just in time for the proclamation of the Hispanic Heritage Month in the United States. That year, the world's attention was focused on a Latin American sportsman. Sammy's performance was taken as a message of congratulations for all Hispanics.

A Mexican fan answered it.

The following day, Fabián Pérez Mercado, born in Tijuana and working as a supervisor in a San Diego bakery, went with his wife and their two sons to see Sammy. He caught the ball that was Sammy's 63rd home run and returned it in a great demonstration of camaraderie. Fabián, his wife and their two kids kissed the ball, and then two-year old Carlos Fabián handed it over to Sammy.

"Viva la República Dominicana, Viva el Béisbol"-

Fabián shouted, and that was perhaps the only

moment in which a Mexican shouted Vivas without saying "Viva Méeejico."

On Sunday, September 20th, with the soundtrack of Superman as a background, Sammy jogged around Wrigley Field's diamond, greeting his fans. He stopped between third base and home plate. There were his teammates, his mother Mireya, his brothers, his wife and children. Hall of Fame member Juan Marichal, who was the Dominican Republic's Minister of Sports at the time, the American baseball commissioner, Bud Selig, and the Cubs' general manager, Ed Lynch were also present.

The Dominican and American flags got confused in that joyful afternoon: after all, they have exactly the same colors. That day, Chicago paid tribute to its new sports hero: Sammy Sosa, now a worldwide celebrity.

Homers Vs. Hearts

On Tuesday, September 22nd, he got the news.

Hurricane Georges literally combed the Dominican Republic; blowing away a good part of Consuelo, San Pedro de Macorís, San Luis and other parts of the country. The death toll was unknown at the time, and the damage to the country's economy was very high. Thousands of people lost their lives. Many survivors lost their means of making a living, and even their homes. Sammy set out to coordinate and ask for donations for the victims. The day the hurricane struck was a difficult one for him. Phone communication with the Dominican Republic was almost impossible, and there was no complete information about the situation of his grandmother, still living in Consuelo. That night, his personal dilemma was reflected in his performance: no home runs.

The following day, Wednesday, September 23rd, had something special for Puerto Rico, Roberto Clemente and Peruchin Cepeda's homeland. That day they were commemorating the 130th anniversary of the Grito de Lares, which was the most important unsuccessful attempt to gain the island's independence from Spain. Sammy celebrated it in County Stadium in Milwaukee, where he hit a homer in the fifth inning and another in the sixth, adding up to 65 and tying with McGwire once again. During five consecutive visits that both players made to that stadium, over a quarter of a million fans showed up, the highest attendance in the entire history of the stadium.

On Friday, at the Astrodome in Houston, Sammy sent a pitch over the fence in a 420 feet trip into history. It was his 66th home run. For forty five minutes, he was the king and indisputable world leader in homers. That very evening at Busch Stadium in Saint Louis, McGwire hit his 66th and, in the following days he hit two more homers in each of two games, ending the season with 70 and Sammy with 66.

The American press talked about McGwire as the "winner of the competition" for the home run record. If there is to be a competition, there needs to be at least two individuals chasing the same goal. From the very beginning, Sammy said that his goal was to help his team win and push McGwire to break the records; he was not competing.

The media promoted a non-existent competition; that was the only way in which they could end up with a "winner" or a hero. While the American press talked about McGwire as the "winner," the Dominican press said that the red-haired Californian won the home run record, while Sammy conquered the hearts of the fans.

EXTRA
Inning

Archivos Dominicanos

Sammy Sosa with president Leonel Fernández, while being decorated with the Orden de Duarte, Sánchez y Mella.

Top of the Tenth

The Adventure Continues

Every year Sammy repeated his ritual distribution of gifts and money among friends and relatives. He is one of those rare beings who, after experiencing the joy of receiving everything from life, discovers new pleasure in improving the lives of fellow human beings. He demonstrated that during the winter of 1997, flying out of the warm Caribbean to the frozen north, to dress up as Santa Claus and tour many American hospitals, distributing toys to sick children.

They called him Sammy Claus.

His professional path was very rough, filled with ups and downs, but once he got to the Cubs, he started to rise in a more or less vertical direction. As his income rose, he increased the gifts and money to friends and relatives. By the end of the 1998 season, he had harvested more success and popularity than just about any other player in baseball history. He broke many old records and established new ones.

And he set new standards for sportsmanship.

After building the bridge that reunited fans and players during the season, now he was about to build another one. On the one end there were his old friends in the Dominican Republic who, due to the hurricane, needed him more than ever. Hurricane Georges wiped out many shantytowns and slums on the outskirts of San Pedro. Thousands of families ended up homeless and became refugees in the homes of friends and relatives. Many of them were Sammy's old buddies, those he spent time with in the Parque Duarte and the old building across from the Tetelo Vargas Stadium. Among those harmed by the storm were people Sammy knew for years, people who never asked him for anything, but now needed everything. That year the list of gifts and money had the potential of being very, very long.

On the other hand, to do this on his own would have been difficult. So he asked for support from his American fans. There he constructed the other end of the bridge: Sammy connected Americans' goodwill with the suffering and needs of the Dominicans victimized by the hurricane's rage. By the time the Atlanta Braves took the Cubs out of the season, Sammy had the public sending small donations to the Cubs' Community Relations Office.

He went to Chicago's City Hall, to private clubs and to every place where he could hold out his baseball cap asking for donations. In a few weeks, the Cubs Office received almost a half a million dollars in small checks from the fans.

The fundraising did not stop there, but kept going as far as Sammy's stardom could take it. A team of Major League players flew to Japan for a short exhibition series, and, as expected, Sammy was in the group. In Japan he was the attraction of the series and its MVP. Taking advantage of this opportunity for his fundraising campaign, he was given thousands of pre-built houses for the Dominican families left homeless after the hurricane.

Back To Home

Sammy arrived in New York City, the place with the largest Dominican population outside their country, on a Friday to fulfill a busy agenda. The first thing he did was go to Mass at Saint Patrick's Cathedral. John Cardinal O'Connor presented him with the John Paul II Award, commemorative of the 20th year of the Pope's reign. From the Cathedral, he went to visit sick children in a couple of metro New York hospitals. At the first stop, Saint Clare's Hospital in Manhattan, New York Governor George Pataki and Jackie Robinson's widow, Mrs. Rachel Robinson, waited for him. In a humble ceremony, he was honored as the first recipient of the Jackie Robinson Award for his outstanding performance on and off the baseball diamond.

That same afternoon New York's Mayor, Rudolph Giulliani, whose police had attempted to stop the Sosamanía in the summer, awarded Sammy a recognition in the Cannon of the Heroes, the most privileged place for a parade in New York City. Luminaries such as the Pope are among those chosen for the honor. The previous parade was for Senator and astronaut John Glenn. He traveled seven million miles to and from space on a NASA mission at age 77, becoming the first Grandfather to ascend to the heavens and come back to earth.

Sammy's parade in the Cannon of the Heroes was another reason for a feud between Mayor Giulliani and Hispanics in New York City. The people wanted the parade in Washington Heights, the Dominican barrio in Northern Manhattan. The mayor, on the other hand, wanted to take political advantage of the opportunity to be associated with one of the most popular persons in the country. He decided to make it a big event and took Sammy to Cannon of the Heroes. Many of Sammy's Dominican fans disagreed, but they would not leave Sammy on his own with Giuliani, and flooded the parade.

The mayor presented Sammy with a symbolic Key to the City. Sammy immediately turned to the public, mainly Dominicans, and told them: "This key that the mayor offered me belongs to you guys, because you are the ones who live here."

As Jackie Robinson did in similar situation, Sammy took advantage of the opportunity to state his desire for better treatment for his community. He expressed his hope that his performance in the game and the recognition given to him would change the negative perception that some people have about many Latin Americans, and Dominicans in particular. Then he made the announcement that everyone was waiting for:

"I am not leaving the city without visiting Washington Heights."

The crowd exploded in applause. He left the Cannon, went to his hotel, changed clothes, and that night he was in The Bronx, at Yankee Stadium's mound. He threw out the first pitch to begin the World Series, at the same stadium where he debuted and connected for his first home run nine years earlier.

The following day he kept his word.

It was Sunday, October 18, when he visited Washington

Heights and toured the streets greeting the crowd that turned out to see him. He then attended a private fundraising breakfast where people paid $500 to eat with him. The money went to the relief fund for the hurricane's victims. By Monday, it was announced that he was unanimously chosen Most Valuable Player of the National League, becoming the second Dominican to win that distinction. Then he attended various fundraising events and boarded a private jet that took him back home to the Dominican Republic on Tuesday, October 20th.

The Return Of The Hero

Arriving in the Dominican Republic, Sammy was received with a huge tribute, never before rendered to any figure in the history of the country. People from all walks of Dominican life, political parties, churches and all sports organizations, waited for him at the airport and provided him with a national hero's welcome.

President Leonel Fernandez headed the receiving committee at the airport. Then Sammy was presented with every award and recognition that can be given. From the Duarte Sánchez and Mella Medal of Honor, the highest offered by the Dominican Republic, to a doctorate, Honoris Causa, by Pontifica Universidad Católica Madre y Maestra.

In the Dominican Republic, as in New York City, there were honors invented just to present to him. After countless ceremonies, speeches and gatherings, Sammy invested his time in supervising the construction of a children's clinic in San Pedro de Macorís. He toured many sites to verify that donations were going to the needy; he also checked out the damage caused by the hurricane.

Oh, Consuelo!

Hurricane Georges uprooted the majority of the village's giant laurel trees and took down one of the rusted chimneys of the old sugar factory. The moneylenders went bankrupt forever, and the workers replaced them by becoming lenders themselves. After Sammy's success in 1998, most of them carried around $16,000 Dominican pesos, about $1,000 dollars in their pocket all the time. It was money they could not possibly spend because no one accepted it. That is why they had it in abundance. That money was contained in the promissory notes that the factory gave out so that they would get paid sometime in the future. When the company went bankrupt, the workers carried notes in their pockets indicating that the company owed them many months' back wages. The workers were the ones who "loaned" to the factory; they worked with the hope they would get paid some day.

This is a matter of faith and, therefore, beyond reason.

Once, they burst into a protest demanding their back wages and the police repressed the demonstrators, forcing them back to their non-paying jobs. They became people without options, who literally made a living out of their backyards. The once profitable factory from the times of Mr. Kilbourne, that made enough money to build homes for its workers, faded away.

After over 37 years of looting it, the politicians finally succeeded; the company was bankrupt and ended up in the hands of private investors, as part of the trendy privatization wave that swept through Latin America. Their houses, built thanks to community unity under Padre José's leadership, ended up having "baby houses." The majority of them have smaller houses built in their yards. The sons and daughters of the workers built houses in their parents' backyards and there they live. Most of them work in San Pedro's Industrial Free Zone and share the little money they make with their parents and their own families.

San Pedro's Team: Las Estrellas

The 1998-99 baseball season in the Dominican Republic was the first one, since 1969 in which the Estrellas Orientales did not lose. They did not win either, because they did not play. Their fans, now evolved into mourners, were more pitiful than ever, since they did not even have a bad team to suffer and cry for. Hurricane Georges trashed the Estadio Tetelo Vargas, and due to that, the team did not participate in the national baseball season.

A Hero, In Two Countries?

While Sammy was involved in building a children's clinic and supervising the distribution of donations, President Bill Clinton invited him to the White House. He thanked him for the honor and asked the president to reschedule the invitation because he was too busy at the time. Shortly after, First Lady Hillary Rodham Clinton visited the Dominican Republic and met with Sammy to coordinate donations for the children's clinic he was building in San Pedro.

By January, Clinton invited Sammy again, but this time it was not to the White House, but to the U.S. Congress. Maiky was one of the President's guests the night he presented his State of the Union address before Congress.

That night, Sammy was recognized in the hall of the institution with the greatest assembly of political power on the planet, by the politically most powerful man on earth. During his speech, Clinton, who was trying to clean up his public image after his sexual scandal, recognized many people he defined as "heroes." Among them was Mrs. Rosa Parks, the African-American woman who in 1955 was arrested because she refused to give up her seat to a white man on a bus. That was the law and the "social custom" of the time. With her refusal, Mrs. Parks ignited the Civil Rights movement and the definitive fight against racial discrimination that was continued by Martin Luther King Jr., Malcom X, and others. That night Clinton also honored military heroes.

While speaking about Sammy, he said that because of his performance, on and off the baseball diamond, he was a "hero in two nations."

Clinton was wrong.

Sammy is a baseball hero, and the universality of that sport gives his heroism a broader reach. He has been received as a hero in many Latin American countries; his stardom shines over sovereign nations and it seems to circle the globe along with the sun. It started out in San Pedro de Macorís, a town hanging on the Caribbean shore where the Higuamo River flows into the sea. In the Dominican Republic, San Pedro is known as the *"city of the beautiful sunsets."* During late afternoon hours in San Pedro, the horizontal sun shines over the sweet and salty waters with different shades of colors. In that very place, where the river ends and the sea begins, every afternoon, the Higuamo River, the Caribbean Sea, and the sun invent new colors and new shades in old colors, in San Pedro's sunsets. Then the sun dives into the sea, as if it died, but in fact it is attending the sunrise in the other side of the planet, in Japan, the land of the rising sun, where Sammy is also a hero.

Archivos Dominicanos

With First Lady Hillary Rodham Clinton.

Bottom of the Tenth

Past, Present and Future

Good and extraordinary things happen in fantasies and, when they become reality, they are part of the past. We hear the stories about "good old days," explaining how wonderful things were during years long gone by.

Roger Maris set his record 37 years ago. Babe Ruth made history 71 years ago, way back when our grandparents were grandchildren. Those records were set in such a remote past that they can almost be considered fantasy.

The 1998 season was a gift for this generation.

It happened in our present, and no one knows when and if it will ever be repeated. It took baseball 34 years, between Ruth and Maris, to set a new record, and the difference was just one homer. From Maris to 1998, the United States waited 37 years for an American player to set a new record and, as soon as that happened, it took Sammy, a Dominican player, a couple of days to tie it and break it.

Sammy had a season of wonders, one of those that will give us material for bedtime stories to tell our children and grandchildren. For them, it will be part of our generation's "good old days" and it may sound like fantasy. During the last 90 days of the 1998 season, Sammy had the opportunity to be part of something much larger than himself. He experienced feelings that will take him years to get in touch with and express in words.

The Past

The 20th century started with U.S. military occupation in many Latin American countries but, by the century's end, something that no one could have imagined is occurring. Latin Americans invaded the United States.

Today more than 35 million Hispanics live in this country. Between 1960 and 1970, there was great criticism in Latin America of what was being called the "cultural penetration of American Imperialism." The 1990's, witnessed new and effective invaders, those who control territories, who spread their culture and increase their political power. These are the Latin Americans in the United States.

There is not one important city in the United States where Spanish is not as widely spoken as in any Latin American capital. The U.S., before the year 2000 Census, was the fifth-largest Spanish speaking country in the world. Salsa and merengue are controlling a good part of the American musical environment. Latin American movie productions are more and more popular and successful. Spanish radio and TV networks have more audiences all across the U.S. than could have been anticipated a few years ago. Shortly after Sammy's 1998 outstanding performance, two of the country's most popular artists are Ricky Martin and Jennifer López, both Hispanics.

The peaceful invasion of Latin Americans has been more successful than all the U.S. military deployment in the region, and has achieved unbelievable results. The 1996 Democratic National Convention, where President Bill Clinton was chosen for re-election, started with Spanish greetings. Today the candidates with the greatest appeal in any political race list their command of the Spanish language as one of their assets.

Latin American influence has been the strongest in one of the most sensitive areas in American contemporary society. For Americans, baseball is a matter of national pride, and today the heroes of this country's national sport aren't "All Americans" they are "All Latin Americans."

The end of the 1998 baseball season confirmed this.

The Most Valuable Players in both the American and the National Leagues were two Latin Americans players, Juan "Igor" González, a Puerto Rican, and Sammy Sosa, a Dominican. Certainly, the new generation of American leaders is growing up inspired by Latin American heroes.

What will be the consequences of this?

Sammy Sosa's influence continues to grow, not by accumulating home runs, but by sharing, and helping to reduce human suffering. His is a new kind of heroism based on love of humankind and community service. If these values inspire our future leaders, there is no doubt that the world will be a better place again, thanks to baseball.

Predicting the future is a very risky business, but with baseball we can anticipate that positive things can come out of this new trend; a quick look back supports that optimism.

In detail it is difficult to predict, but the consequences will be beneficial for the United States, for Latin Americans in this country, and those south of the border.

No one knows what can happen.

No one could have predicted that invaders and invaded were going to end up playing baseball as good brothers during the American occupation of the Dominican Republic at the beginning of the 20th Century. It was difficult to anticipate that it would be through baseball that the process of desegregation was going to start in the Uni-ted States. After Jackie Robinson and Larry Doby, who broke baseball's color barrier in the early 1950's, came Rosa Parks, Martin Luther King Jr., numerous protests, marchers and sweeping civil rights legislation. Baseball keeps being as unpredictable as it has always been, creating opportunities for people to get together in ways they could not have imagined.

The White House's local team, the Baltimore Orioles, traveled to Havana to play in an exhibition series. Clinton sent his very own home team to play for Fidel Castro. Afterwards, the Cuban leader responded to Clinton's gesture by sending the Cuban National team to Baltimore. There were protests from the extremist Cuban exiles, but when the umpire said "Play Ball," all Cubans, those against and those in favor of the Revolution, came together as brothers for the very first time in almost forty years of separation. Baseball reunited the Cuban Family and bridged the gap between the White House and the Palacio de la Revolución.

Baseball keeps on going, and amazes us by performing big miracles.

The Future

The one who compares himself with others will always find people both above and below him. In the past, when Sammy made those comparisons, everyone was above him, economically and socially. In the old abandoned building where he threw himself on the floor at night to fight the mosquitoes, when he looked down, only the floor was under him, and it was very, very close to his eyes. The whole world was above him; he could not get any lower.

Now he lives in a 55th floor penthouse with a panoramic view of Chicago, one of the most interesting cities in the world, and of majestic Lake Michigan, the sixth largest lake on the planet. Today he has many things to see when he looks down; he could never have imagined anything like this, no wonder one of his favorite expressions is "unbelievable."

His whole life's story is simply "unbelievable."

That is why it should not surprise us if more "unbelievable" things keep coming for him. In just a couple of days, he broke a record untouched for almost four decades. Sammy has a clear history of setting and breaking records. A brief retrospective can shed light on this.

In 1993, he became "Mr. 30 x 30," and the following year something curious happened. After only 105 games of the 1994 season, a players' strike interrupted it. Sammy had 25 homers and 22 stolen bases. During the 50 remaining games, there is no doubt he could have gotten five more home runs and stolen eight more bases. That would have been his second year in a row as "Mr. 30 x 30," because the third year was in 1995, when he had 36 homers and 34 stolen bases. Taking this into account, it should not surprise us if Sammy keeps doing things as "unbelievable" as his own story.

No one in his early life of poverty and instability could have imagined that Sammy would wind up living where he lives today. From up there, at the top of his sporting career and in one of the highest places in which a modern human being can live, Sammy has become, without any doubt, an "unbelievable" star.

He also became an advertising model, promoting a variety of goods and services. In the Dominican Republic, he offered advice about the best way to invest; he also gives household guidance: recommending the best washing machine that will fit the needs of the most demanding housewife. In the United States, he has been in McDonald's advertisements, portrayed as one of the people most American kids want to be. He also promotes huge franchises such as Kmart, and his pictures illustrate cereal boxes.

Strangely enough, when Sammy connected for his 62nd homer, it is said that someone put a replica of a cereal box with a picture of his hero, Roberto Clemente, next to his locker. Today, Sammy has repeated and passed most of Clemente's achievements. He has given the same demonstration of human solidarity and sensibility as Clemente did.

Life has another gift for him. Clemente's children want Sammy to play the role of their father in a movie about the life of the Puerto Rican star.

After following in the footsteps of his hero in real life, he is now invited to enter the fantasy life of the movie to embody him. It is unknown how many, if any other human beings, have ever been so fortunate in life.

The Last Out, Beware!

Any street child, dirty, half-naked, visibly underfed and sick, has all the conditions needed to be a Sammy Sosa. Perhaps he only needs a bit of affection and attention.

Appendix

A Free Fall

When the fans were expecting to see him perform his slow motion jump, as if defying gravity while celebrating a home run, he was praying for quite the opposite. In silence he begged, "earth, please open up and swallow me down." Or perhaps he should have, because that would have been a pretty reasonable way out of the calamity in which his wonderful life was collapsing into.

Newspapers were printing stories about how his family was falling apart. One day that ball, flying at around 100 miles per hour, blew away his protective helmet exactly over his left ear. And death whispered to him *"Cucurrucucú," tú.*

When his bat broke and the umpire found cork in it that was the last spin in the whirlpool that was spinning out of control, threatening to destroy his life, family, fame and fortune. The only thing untouched, up to that moment, was his professional integrity, and that was now covered by the shadow of public doubt.

The spirits of fortune had deserted him or, if they were still there, they were working against him.

Sammy Sosa was like a sailboat adrift, blown away by ominous winds in the sea of uncertainty. After he rose very high, he was descending in a free fall over a strange and bottomless abyss.

A few days after the corked bat incident, I addressed the students of Union High School in Grand Rapids, Michigan. Sammy had already taken responsibility for his mistake and offered a public apology. It was still not clear if he had other corked bats in his possession.

I told the students that his was an example to learn from; accept responsibility for your mistakes and ask for an apology.

That is very uncommon in this country.

In those days there was a sort of collective feeling that the country had suffered another big moral set back. One president lied about sex, another about war. The Roman Catholic Church, by denying the sexual misconduct of many priest, also lied. Corporate scams, such as Enron and insider trade scandals in the stock market, like Martha Stewart's case, were in the every day news.

The country needed an example of integrity.

Church, Government and Corporate America had lost its moral authority.

In that environment of collective disbelief, Sammy said that he got confused and took the wrong bat, the corked one, that he had used in batting practices to thrill the fans.

Many people wanted to believe him.

He had to prove his integrity.

All together 76 bats from his locker, and five from the Baseball Hall of Fame, with which he had broken records in 1998, were scanned with X Rays.

Not one was corked.

There is still a missing part of the corked bat. Today there are two big mysteries in Chicago: the final destiny of Al Capone's valise, and of the missing part of Sammy's corked bat. Both pieces are on permanent exhibition in the museum of lost and invisible objects.

Sammy's integrity was already under question; he was under a federal investigation suspected of one of the felonies more severely punished in the United States.

Tax Scam

Benjamin Franklin said it, and it is real: "In this world nothing can be said to be certain, except death and taxes."

Sammy's problems with the Internal Revenue Service (IRS) started in June 1998, when someone suggested he create a foundation for charity and for tax exemptions purposes.

He loved the idea.

But no one explained to him the laws and rules of philanthropy. He had, and perhaps still has, no idea whatsoever, about the existence of something called the National

Charities Information Bureau. Of course, he had totally ignored the standards for public charities such as his foundation.

No one explained to him that besides obeying the law, he must follow some strict unwritten rules as well.

No one explained to him that there should be no financial relationships between his personal business and his foundation.

No one explained to him that the members of his board of directors should not be employees, or profit from the organization.

No one explained to him a fundamental rule that need not be in the books, because every player in the Major League of Philanthropy follows it as a divine commandment: Appoint only people you absolutely trust to key positions.

Even if he was told these and other things, Sammy doesn't have the educational background to understand, process and manage these concepts.

Very few educated Americans understand the non-profit world, and Sammy didn't even make it to junior high school. For him it may well be more complicated than rocket science and brain surgery combined; or like asking him to decode the science fiction, mythology and real science behind *Deep Space 9* and *The Lord of the Rings*.

Sammy set up his foundation in Miami and, as it was to be expected, a Cuban got a key position. Sammy appointed musician Arturo Sandoval secretary, a position whose very name defines it as the depositary of secrets.

Bill Chase, an old friend of Sammy's who lived in one of Sammy's houses in Coral Springs, Florida, was appointed president. Dana Kaufman, Sammy's accountant, sat on the board, Sammy was the third member and Sandoval the fourth.

It is necessary to have five members on the board of public charities; the Sammy Sosa Charitable Foundation only had four. It is against the regulations that any board member be beholden to the philanthropic organization, and all the board members, except Sandoval, were under Sammy's control.

Sandoval proved he wasn't worthy of "absolute trust" because he called in the IRS on Sammy. He, the depositary of the foundation's secrets, told Fortune magazine that Sammy was handling the organization as his personal piggy bank. The IRS started an investigation into the Sammy Sosa Charitable Foundation and found many wrongdoings.

Including very ugly things.

The Numbers

Up until the year 2000, when the IRS started its probe, Sammy had only made one donation to his foundation. It was "Plaza 30 x 30" in San Pedro de Macorís, an anthological business failure, a shopping center that never took off.

And the numbers didn't add up.

Back in 1996, when the building was dedicated, with President Leonel Fernández as a witness, Sammy said it was a $50.0 million pesos investment, around $5.0 million dollars at the time exchange rate. In 1998 it was valued, for donation purposes, at $2.7 million, taking an apparent $2.3 million loss.

On the spot Sammy got a tax deduction of at least $1.3 million, but the building's real value was and continued to be a mystery.

Its initial budget was $28.0 million pesos, equal to a little over $2.7 million dollars at the then current exchange rate, but in a few days the numbers skyrocketed to the $50.0 million he finally claimed. It was said that the builder and one of Sammy's brothers shared responsibility —and perhaps more than that— for the increased budged.

Now the shopping center belonged to the foundation, but Sammy's sisters kept using it as family property. The "Plaza 30 x 30" kept being a source of conflict in the Dominican Republic, in the United States the foundation has other problems.

In the year 2000 Sammy still had not made any significant cash donation to his own foundation, but the organization had spent a considerable amount of money.

Where did the money come from?

At the end of the enchanted summer of 1998, Hurricane Georges devastated the Dominican Republic, and Sammy's hometown, San Pedro de Macorís, was hit hard.

Fans of all ages, including children sending in their weekly allowances made generous donation to the fouda-tion.

Mark McGwire pitched in a $100,000 donation in 1999. The foundation's 1998 tax return claimed to have sent only $82,481 in aid to the Dominican Republic.

What did they do with the money?

Mr. Chase admitted to Fortune magazine that he used charity money to buy a new sports car for José, Sammy's brother. Also that they spent money on "consultant" fees and other things unrelated to the foundation's mission.

"Someone has to clarify with Sammy that he cannot take charitable contributions from the United States and directly deposit [them] into his business account in the Dominican Republic," Sandoval said.

He was the secretary and should not have pocketed $4,000 a year in "consulting fees" while being on the board. Chase suspended Sandoval's consulting contract and locked him out of the foundation's offices.

Adam Katz, Sammy's agent, "virtually" assured that there was no "impropriety," in the handling of the foundation. He promised to "clean up" the situation in Miami. You only "clean" what is dirty and Mr. Katz didn't explained how far his cleaning would go.

Domingo Dahuajre, Sammy's advisor and the person who runs the foundation in the Dominican Republic, confirmed that the IRS banned them from accepting donations, but the ban had its limitations.

"That is over there, in the United States, here in the Dominican Republic, here we continue to accept them," he said while banging his right-hand knuckles on the desk.

Sammy's success in Major League Baseball did not translate into Major League Philanthropy. A kind heart and a gentle spirit can't go very far in the dog eat dog world. And the people around him may not be doing the best job they can.

Here is an important lesson.

Even on the top of fame and fortune, education is still fundamental; the higher up we move the more we need it.

Up there the lack of education has devastating effects.

Sammy's name is involved in something with all the characteristics of a transnational tax scam. It is almost certain that the guy has no clue of how he got there.

While the IRS was digging into Sammy's books, the newspapers in the Dominican Republic were publishing ugly things. So ugly that he may have been forced to ask himself the question every man wants to avoid asking, for fear of an affirmative answer.

Is My Wife Unfaithful?

Sergio Vargas is a Dominican merengue superstar. He recorded a song in which a lover laments that his beloved one abandoned him and married another man, leaving the door open for reconciliation.

Many Dominicans decided that the lyrics were written by Sergio to Sonia Sosa, Sammy's wife. Words made it into the newspapers that something went on, or may well still be going on, or could have gone on between Sonia and Sergio Vargas.

Why?

Because Sonia was a model in Dominican TV when Sergio Vargas was one the most desired men on the land. This may not prove anything, but it turned out to be excellent fuel for gossip.

The rumor spread like an infectious disease, highly transmittable. That merengue broke sales records. If there was or was not anything between Sergio and Sonia, before or after she married Sammy, that became absolutely irrelevant. The seed of doubt was planted in public. Inside Sammy's head only God knew what was going on.

And then, the next shoe fell.

In May 2003 Banco Intercontinental (Baninter), the Dominican bank where Sammy had his savings, sank. And there is no deposit insurance in the Dominican Republic. His money disappeared in an instant, but that wasn't all.

The worse was yet to come.

With all those things on his mind, Sammy didn't see the ball, traveling at around 100 mph, that blew away his protective helmet, right over his left ear in June 2003, he just didn't see it. The helmet saved his life, but death licked his ear.

By then he fully understood Franklin's insights about the certainty of death and taxes.

The Great Survivor

At that point in time in Sammy's life, the corked bat was nothing but a great insignificance. Studies about the physics of corked bats states that they are as irrelevant as the chemical effects of placebos in pharmaceutical experiments. They remain, nevertheless, strictly prohibited in baseball, and many players think they really make a difference.

In July 1994, Albert Belle was suspended for using a corked bat.

Houston Astros' Billy Hatcher was suspended for 10 games because of a corked bat, and Norm Cash, from the Detroit Tigers, confessed that he used them.

In 1974 New York Yankees third baseman, Craig Nettles' bat broke, and they found something called "SuperBats" in it.

Len Dykstra from the New York Mets confessed in his book "Nails" that he used corked bats in the minor leagues. Wilton Guerrero, from the L.A. Dodgers, was suspended from eight games and fined $1,000 because of corked bats.

Sammy paid a fine, and for two weeks he was suspended. At the end of the season, had 40 home runs.

With the corked bat Sammy may have touched the bottom of the pond and, since cork does not sink, he is now floating again on the surface. The incident was thrown away in the wastebasket of memory.

It was forgotten.

Before becoming a great home run hitter, Sammy was an outstanding athlete in the game of survival.

We, the people, turn these ordinary fellows into celebrities, pay them a delusional amount of money, and annoint them "superior" to us. Then they become the "role models" for our children. We expect them to behave in ways we are not willing to demand from our children, or to teach them with the examples of our own behavior.

To expect someone else to do the work for us is at the very least irresponsible.

Celebrities can't be our children's role models. Because they don't know how to, and don't have to, and they may not want to, and above all, they have their own children. They have their own difficulties, and are usually quite busy making money, protecting themselves and waiting for the next shoe to fall.

They can support family and education values. To read the story of their lives, in this case Sammy Sosa, can inspire, enrich and educate the children. To guide them and provide them with models is the shared and non-transferable responsibility of parents, educators and the whole community.

Letter to Danny Almonte

The Dominican Baseball Gold Rush

Sammy Sosa's talent contributed to reviving Major League Baseball, and yours did the same for the Little Leagues. The little players of today, and the still unborn that will play tomorrow, are in debt to you, for calling the world's attention to their great small world.

Many fortunes were, are and will continue to be made on the basis of your talent. You are like a children's version of King Midas.

Everything you touch is turned into gold.

And that may not be the best thing that happened to you, because what is good for business is not necessarily good for you.

There is no money for you because you are still a "minor," but that goes unnoticed when it comes to making money with you, off you.

You were, are and will continue to be exploited, until the last drop of juice is squished out of you.

You have brought light to many things around you.

The United States is a country full of noble people, genuinely concerned about children's welfare. It has an impressive, incredible and effective system to protect the children, but the government refuses to sign an international treaty against child labor.

Many of those who own factories overseas exploit poor children in their own poor countries. Those who control the entertainment industry in the United States exploit the exploitation of the poor children, from here, at a safe distance. The treatment you, as a minor, are getting from certain businesses, is nothing less than child exploitation.

Don't get me wrong, you will see that Americans are a group of quite interesting people. They are not good, they are not bad, they are just who they are; they do a lot of good things, and a lot of bad things, just because. They personalize everything, but you shouldn't personalize what is happening to you.

There is nothing personal against you, you just happen to be a poor, talented child, from a poor country, suspended over a poor immigration status.

Many people are taking advantage of your poverty. Your poverty is part of you, to forget her, is to forget about yourself. Together you will travel through the narrow avenues of the universe, the air, seas and highways. It is better to accept her as a traveling companion that always reminds you where you are coming from. She will never desert you, no matter how many millions you get.

Poverty is faithful.

Never forget your roots.

If you ignore where you are coming from, you will never get to where you are going to; spending your life coming and going to nowhere.

Your story didn't happen in the emptiness; like you, it has its own history.

An Old Story

What happens to you has happened before and continues to happen to many young ball players. Changing your age is like a rite of passage to become a great Dominican baseball player.

Your parents didn't do anything the parents of the majority of our great stars have not done. This was going on long before you or your parents were born.

And Dominicans did not invent this scam.

After Ricardo Carty drove the fans crazy during the 1959 Pan American Amateur Baseball Championship in Chicago, an army of scouts invaded our village, Ingenio Consuelo, looking for similar players. At age 19, Carty stood six feet tall with over 200 pounds of muscles.

The scouts found very good players, but not as young, tall and strong as Carty. Our boys were severely undernourished, they didn't look quite right for their ages. The scouts decided to deliberately reduce their ages by a few years, as a creative way of correcting the signs of poverty expressed in their retarded physical development.

After "fixing" their child's age, the parents would get thousands of dollars on the spot, and if the boy turned out to be good, money would rain over them. The parents only had to produce a birth certificate stating that the kid was between two and four years younger than his real age.

During the Trujillo dictatorship, between 1930 and 1961, in the Dominican Republic organization got confused with repression; after his death, somewhere along the road to democracy, certain illegalities were assumed as civil liberties.

The Dominican Baseball Gold Rush started with false birth certificates. Everyone knew it, but said nothing, because they were busy counting their part of the booty. The government employees got money for "fixing" birth certificates while the parents got a lump sum instantly. The scouts took an outstanding and "younger" player, making more money because he promised a longer professional life.

One hand washed the other and all washed the face. Baseball, as part of the entertainment industry, increased its profits with these players. The real victim of this scam, the fans, were too busy cheering our boys and never really cared about their ages.

They tampered with your age because you have a great deal of talent. You are gifted. But Danny, be careful, because our blessings can became our worse curses.

Poverty and talent dwell in you, the mixing of those elements produces a third unnamed one; the very matter from which big things are made off.

Star You Are

The scouts combed our sugarcane fields looking for young boys. God knows that, as the new target of the scouts, they were over fished and almost driven into extinction; young Dominican boys are an endangered species. "Protective laws" were enacted prohibiting signing them up to play pro ball until they are 16. It was like the law that prohibits taking out of the water fish that has not yet grown to a certain dimension.

Not all fishermen respect those laws; there are Major League teams willing to do anything to get a talented Dominican boy.

In 1996 Tampa Bay signed up a 15 years old child in San Pedro de Macorís, named Josephang Benhard, a nephew of Dominican star Ramón –Moncho– Benhard. Josephang's dad, José Angel –el Feo– was talked into changing his mind, because his son was still a child.

Tampa Bay went to a ridiculous extreme and hired a medical doctor to demonstrate that Josephang was 16. To prove that the family did not know the age of their son was a hard one to pull off, and they lost the case. When Josephang turned 16, his birthday gift was a $1.2 million contract. The Toronto Blue Jays took him under their wings and flew him far away from the sugarcane fields.

After that, there was another high profile case with a child. It is also said that Adrian Beltré, the L.A. Dodgers second baseman, was 15 when he was signed up, and his age was increased to 16. In the scandal, many government employees made money and lost their jobs.

It is true that no one respects the "protective laws", but al least they produce a considerable increase in the "price" of talented Dominican boys.

Any poor Dominican family with a child as talented as you, may well increase his age, get in touch with a scout and get a good bonus. They will then put the child on a plane and pray to the Virgencita de la Altagracia that he becomes the next Sammy Sosa, Pedro Martínez or Alex Rodríguez.

To have a falsified age is an unequivocal sign that you are a star, and Dominicans are not the only ones that do it.

Americans, Too

Many American sports commentators made fun of the scandal surrounding your age, admitting that those things happened all the time when they were kids.

One commentator said that the pitcher of his Little League team once dropped his car keys on the mound. Another one said that his manager banned a player from a game, because he had not shaved in many days.

Your problem wasn't only your age.

Your case was really strange, because it was as if a group of Dominicans were trying to pull off a sting on the same Americans that invented that scam.

It seems to be that tampering with age is no problem, as long as the profits go to those who control the business. In your case they only had their empty hands to cheer you with, because someone else was going to make the money.

Being used to counting money while others cheer, they may have not liked that.

The day you pitched the perfect game, a serious mistake was made. Your team from The Bronx was an American team playing in Williamsport Pennsylvania, an American town. Your team's fans did not wave American flags, they waved Dominican flags.

It was like planting a flag, claiming territory.

It was a very stupid thing to do.

It was the beginning of the scandal.

It was said that you were older than 12.

A private detective was hired to prove you older, but the guy had no access to documents and proved nothing. The organizers of the World Series denied the accusation and even declared the case closed.

Then Rolando Paulino, the manager of your team, did something even more stupid. He showed up in Williamsport with a group of passports and birth certificates. Those documents, in this country, at that level, no one shows them without a court order.

Paulino volunteered the information the private detective couldn't find. The documents he showed were recorded in video. *Sports Illustrated* magazine sent a reporter to your hometown with a copy printed from the video.

They looked at records two years earlier than what the document said, because they knew exactly how those things are done, and they produced another legal document saying you were 14.

They All Used You

Your performance increased the ratings for the Little League World Series' broadcasters. Advertisers got real value for airtime they bought, consumers responded and their sales went up.

Even President George W. Bush said nice things about you, because you were positive publicity. And New York Mayor Michael Bloomberg gave you and your teammates the Keys to the City.

The scandal questioning the honorability of your family was replaced on the front pages by the attacks of September 11. Ironically enough, the investigations of the attack put Dominican ballplayers again in the forefront. Reviewing their immigration documents, it was established that the majority had their ages changed.

No one said anything about this, because to question the honorability of our stars, among the most important in the game, would be an assault on baseball. No one will do that.

If you really were 14 in 2001, by 2005 you will be 18; legally able to sign up, get a bonus and start playing pro ball.

Money will never give you the important things in life. Quite the contrary, after you get money you will need to hire attorneys and accountants. Their job will be to protect you, and yours to protect yourself from them.

Being a Little Leaguer, you are already receiving the treatment of a Big Leaguer celebrity. Do not allow anyone or anything to distract you. As the posthumous song of the Salsa Queen, Celia Cruz said, "hold on tight, and don't ever let go," you are just taking off in a long and exciting journey.

Young, famous, rich and inexperienced is as glamorous as it is dangerous; Danny, you have to be as careful as you can possibly be. You still have to step into the "missteps of early success;" that's your next test. Good luck, you are going to need a lot of it.

Keep your forehead together and always high up, to honor your ancestors, Juan Marichal, Felipe Rojas Alou, Mateo Rojas Alou, Ricardo Carty and many more. Learn from your older brothers, Pedro Martinez, Sammy Sosa, Alex Rodríguez and the grandpa of ballplayers, Julio César Franco.

God and many men have great expectations for you. Your responsibility will be to keep your concentration, discipline, consistency and persistency.

Invest in faith, hope and, above all, in love.

The rest will fall into place.

Don't spend much time feeling sorry for yourself. We all know that what happened to you was not OK, acceptable or decent, but there is an American way of explaining it: "that is the way it is." Which doesn't necessarily means that it is the way it should be or should continue to be.

Without Sammy's talent there would have been lots of unbroken records in Major League Baseball, without yours, the same would have happened in the Little Leagues. You are part of something greater than both of you combined; you are very important messengers, but the message you are to deliver is more important than you.

That message is that poor children, given the right opportunities, can produce advancements in science and technology, arts and humanities, just as Sammy you and many others did in baseball.

That denying equal access to education, health care and other services to poor children is dead wrong.

That by leaving poor children behind, we waste the talents and gifts they have to offer to the wealth of human knowledge.

That by doing so, for sure the world misses important opportunities for advancement in many areas.

That promoting, supporting and nourishing the God-given talents of all the children of the world should be a global priority.

That is the only real hope left for the Human family and the future of the Earth.

Sammy Sosa's

1998 Home Runs

HR	Date	Team/Pitcher	Dist.
1	April, 4	Expos/Valdes	371
2	April, 11	Expos/Telford	350
3	April, 15	Mets/Reed	430
4	April, 23	Padres/Miceli	420
5	April, 24	Dodgers/Valdes	430
6	April, 27	Padres/Hamilton	434
7	May, 3	Cardinals/Polite	370
8	May, 16	Red/Sulivan	420
9	May, 22	Bravos/Maddux	440
10	May, 25	Braves/Millwood	410
11	May, 25	Braves/Cather	420
12	May, 27	Phillies/Winston	460
13	May, 27	Phillies/Gómez	400
14	June, 1	Marlins/Dempster	430
15	June, 1	Marlins/Henriquez	410
16	June, 3	Marlins/Hernández	370
17	June, 5	W. Sox/Parque	370
18	June, 6	W. Sox/Castillo	410
19	June, 7	W. Sox/Baldwin	380
20	June, 8	Twins/Hawkins	340
21	June, 13	Phillies/Portugal	350
22	June, 15	Expos/Eldred	420
23	June, 15	Expos/Eldred	410
24	June, 15	Expos/Eldred	415
25	June, 17	Brewers/Patrick	430
26	June, 19	Phillies/Loewer	380
27	June, 19	Phillies/Loewer	380
28	June, 20	Phillies/Beech	366
29	June, 20	Phiellies/Borland	500
30	June, 21	Phillies/Green	380
31	June, 24	Tigers/Greisinger	390
32	June, 25	Tigers/Moehler	400
33	June, 30	D. Blacks/Embree	364
34	July, 9	Brewers/Juden	432
35	July, 10	Brewers/Karl	428
36	July, 17	Marlins/Ojala	440
37	July, 22	Expos/Batista	365
38	July, 26	Mets/Reed	420
39	July, 27	D.Blacks/Blair	350
40	July, 27	D. Blacks/Embree	420
41	July, 28	D.Blacks/Wolcott	400
42	July, 31	Rockies/Wright	371
43	August, 5	D.Blacks/Benes	374
44	August, 8	Cardinales/Croushore	400
45	August, 10	Gigante/Ortiz	370
46	August, 10	Gigante/Brock	480
47	August, 16	Astros/Bergman	360
48	August, 19	Cardinales/Bottenfield	368
49	August, 21	Gigante/Hershiser	415
50	August, 23	Astros/Lima	440
51	August, 23	Astros/Lima	388
52	August,26	Red/Tomko	438
53	August, 28	Rockies/Thomson	414
54	August, 30	Rockies/Kile	482
55	August, 31	Reds/Tomko	364
56	Sept., 2	Reds/Bere	370
57	Sept., 4	Pirates/Schmidt	400
58	Sept., 5	Pirates/Lawrence	405
59	Sept., 11	Brewers/Pulsipher	435
60	Sept., 12	Brewers/D. L. Santos	430
61	Sept., 13	Brewers/Patrick	480
62	Sept., 13	Brewers/Plunk	480
63	Sept., 16	Padres/Boeringer	434
64	Sept., 23	Brewers/Roque	344
65	Sept., 23	Brewers/Henderson	410
66	Sept., 25	Astros/Lima	420

Sammy Sosa's Career Perfomance

Season	TM	G	AB	R	H	2B	3B	HR	RBI	BB	SO	SB	CS	AVG	OBP	SLG	OPS
1989	CWS	33	99	19	27	5	0	3	10	11	27	7	3	.273	.351	.414	.765
1989	Tex	25	84	8	20	3	0	1	3	0	20	0	2	.238	.238	.310	.548
1989	--	58	183	27	47	8	0	4	13	11	47	7	5	.257	.303	.366	.669
1990	CWS	153	532	72	124	26	10	15	70	33	150	32	16	.233	.282	.404	.686
1991	CWS	116	316	39	64	10	1	10	33	14	98	13	6	.203	.240	.335	.575
1992	ChC	67	262	41	68	7	2	8	25	19	63	15	7	.260	.317	.393	.710
1993	ChC	159	598	92	156	25	5	33	93	38	135	36	11	.261	.309	.485	.794
1994	ChC	105	426	59	128	17	6	25	70	25	92	22	13	.300	.339	.545	.884
1995	ChC	144	564	89	151	17	3	36	119	58	134	34	7	.268	.340	.500	.840
1996	ChC	124	498	84	136	21	2	40	100	34	134	18	5	.273	.323	.564	.887
1997	ChC	162	642	90	161	31	4	36	119	45	174	22	12	.251	.300	.480	.780
1998	ChC	159	643	134	198	20	0	66	158	73	171	18	9	.308	.377	.647	1.024
1999	ChC	162	625	114	180	24	2	63	141	78	171	7	8	.288	.367	.635	1.002
2000	ChC	156	604	106	193	38	1	50	138	91	168	7	4	.320	.406	.634	1.040
2001	ChC	160	577	146	189	34	5	64	160	116	153	0	2	.328	.437	.737	1.174
2002	ChC	150	556	122	160	19	2	49	108	103	144	2	0	.288	.399	.594	.993
2003	ChC	137	517	99	144	22	0	40	103	62	143	0	1	.279	.358	.553	.911
2004*	ChC	68	255	39	68	13	0	20	45	36	69	0	0	.267	.355	.553	.908
Total	--	2080	7798	1353	2167	332	43	559	1495	836	2046	233	106	.278	.349	.547	.896

Until the end of July. Source: ESPN.com

Sammy Sosa and the Baseball Record Books

The 500 Home Run Club

1. Hank Aaron 755
2. Babe Ruth....................714
3. Willie Mays 660
4. Barry Bonds 658
6. Mark McGwire 581
7. Harmon Killebrew....................573
8. Reggie Jackson 561
9. **Sammy Sosa 549***
10. Mike Schmidt....................548
11. Mickey Mantle 536
12. Jimmie Foxx 534
13. Rafael Palmeiro 528
14. Willie McCovey....................521
15 Ted Williams 521
16. Ernie Banks 512
17 Eddie Mathews....................512
18. Melt Ott 511
19. Eddie Murray....................504

* Spring 2004

Major League Records held or Shared by Sammy Sosa

Most 60-Homer Seasons: **3** 1998, 1999, 2001
Most 50-Homer Season: **4**....................1998-2000
(shared with Babe Ruth 1920, 1921/1927 and Mark McGwire 1996-99)
Most Consecutive 50-Homer Season: **4** 1998-2001
(shared with Mark McGwire) 1996-1999)
Most Consecutive 35-Homer/1000-RBI Seasons: **9** 1995-2003
(shared with Jimmie Foxx (1932-1940)
and Rafael Palmeiro (1995-2003
Most Homers, Five-Season Span: **292** 1998-2002
Most Homers, Six-Season Span: **332** 1998-2003
Most Homers, Seven-Season Span: **368** 1996-2002, 1997-2003
Most Homers, Eight-Season Span: **408**....................1996-2003
Most Homers, Nine-Season Span: **444** 1995-2003
Most Homer, Ten-Season Span: **469** 1994-2003
Most Total Bases, Four-Season Span: **1,621** 1998-2001

Most 3-Homer Games, Career: **6** ....(shared with Jonny Mize)
Most Multi-Homer Games, Season: 11
(shared with Hank Greenberg 1938)
Most 3-Homer Games, Season: **3**...2001
Most Ballparks Homered in, Season: **18** 1998
(shared with Mike Piazza 2000)
Most Extra-Base Hits, Right Handed Batter, Season: **103** 2000
(shared with Hank Greenberg 1937 and Albert Belle 1995)
Most International Walks, Right Handed Batter, Season: **37** 2001
Most Homer, Any Month: **20** ....June 1998
Most Homer, June: **20**...1998
Most Homers, October: **5**..2001
(shared with Riuchie Sexson 2001)
Mot Homers, 30-Day Span: **21**...5/25-6/23/98
Most Homers, 10 Day Span: **9** 5/26-6/7/98. 6/12-6/21/98
Grand Slams, Consecutive Games....7/27-7/28/98 (shared with many)
Most 3-Run Homers, Game: **3** 8/10/02
(shared with Walker Cooper 7/6/49)
Homers in Three Consecutive Innings....................................8/10/02
(shared with five others)
Most Homers, Innings: **2** 5/16/96
(shared with many)

National League Records Held or Shared by Sammy Sosa
THE ABOVE PLUS...
Most Consecutive 40 Homer Seasons: **6** 1998-2003
Most Consecutive 100-RBI Seasons: **9**.................................1995-2003
Most 150-Plus RBI Seasons: 2 1998-2001
(shared with Hack Wilson 1020-1930)
Most Homers, Three Season Span: **179** 1998-2000
Most Homer in Four Season Span: **243** 1998-2001
Most Homers, August: **17**..2001
(shared with Willie Mays 1965)
Most Homers, Consecutive Seris: **15** 1998
Most Homers, Sunday-Saturday Calendar Week: **8…6** ..../14-6/20/98
(shared with three others)
Most RBI, consecutive Games: **14** 8/10-8/11/02

ALL OF THE ABOVE PLUS
Most 30-Homer Seasons: **10** 1993, 1995, 2003

Most Multiple-Homer Games, Career: 62
Most Homer-Season: **66** 1998
Most Extra-Base Hits, Season: **103**..2001
Most Total Bases Season: **425** 2001
Highest Slugging Percentage, Season: **.737** 2001
Most Homers, Wrigley Fields, Season: **35**.......................................1998
Most Homers, Road, Season: **31**...1998
Strikeouts, Career: 1,682
Strikeouts, Season: **174** 1997
Consecutive Game Homer Streak: 5 games..........................6/3-6/8/98
(shared with two others)
Homers, Three Consecutive Games: **5** 6/19-6/21/98, 8/10-8/12/02
(shared with two others)
Most Hits, Consecutive At-Bat: **9** 6/20-7/293
Most Hits, Game: **6**...................................7/2/93 (shared with several)
Most Homer, Game: **3** ....Six Times (shared with many)
Most Homer, Inning: **2**..5/16/96 - 7th
(shared with Mark Betlhorn 8/29/02 – 4th)
Most RBI, Game: **9** 8/10/02
(shared with Heinie Zimmerman)